FAMILIES
AND
HEALTH

FAMILY STUDIES TEXT SERIES

Series Editor: RICHARD J. GELLES, *University of Rhode Island*
Series Associate Editor: ALEXA A. ALBERT, *University of Rhode Island*

This series of textbooks is designed to examine topics relevant to a broad view of family studies. The series is aimed primarily at undergraduate students of family sociology and family relations, among others. Individual volumes will be useful to students in psychology, home economics, counseling, human services, social work, and other related fields. Core texts in the series cover such subjects as theory and conceptual design, research methods, family history, cross-cultural perspectives, and life course analysis. Other texts will cover traditional topics, such as dating and mate selection, parenthood, divorce and remarriage, and family power. Topics that have been receiving more recent public attention will also be dealt with, including family violence, later life families, and fatherhood.

Because of their wide range and coverage, Family Studies Texts can be used singly or collectively to supplement a standard text or to replace one. These books will be of interest to both students and professionals in a variety of disciplines.

Volumes in this series:

William J. Doherty
and
Thomas L. Campbell

FAMILIES
AND
HEALTH

FAMILY STUDIES
TEXT SERIES **10**

For information address:

SAGE Publications, Inc.
2111 West Hillcrest Drive
Newbury Park, California 91320

SAGE Publications Inc.   SAGE Publications Ltd.
275 South Beverly Drive   28 Banner Street
Beverly Hills   London EC1Y 8QE
California 90212   England

SAGE PUBLICATIONS India Pvt. Ltd.
M-32 Market
Greater Kailash I
New Delhi 110 048 India

Printed in the United States of America

Library of Congress Cataloging-in-Publication Data

Doherty, William J. (William Joseph), 1945-
    Families and health / William J. Doherty and Thomas L. Campbell.
        p.   cm. — (Family studies text series ; v. 10)
    Bibliography: p.
    Includes indexes.
    ISBN 0-8039-2992-7   ISBN 0-8039-2993-5 (pbk.)
    1. Family—health and hygiene.   2. Sick—Family relationships.
3. Social medicine.   I. Campbell, Thomas L. (Thomas Lothrop)
II. Title.   III. Series.
    [DNLM: 1. Family.   WA 308 D655f]
RA418.5.F3D64   1988
306.8'7—dc19
DNLM/DLC   87-28600
for Library of Congress   CIP

To
Leah Doherty
and
Sally Trafton

Contents

Acknowledgments

WE THANK RICHARD GELLES for inviting us to write this volume and for providing prompt and encouraging feedback along the way. We also thank Lorne Becker, Geoffrey Leigh, and Patricia Tomlinson for their very helpful comments on the first draft. Susan McDaniel was an early supporter and critic of this project, who helped set the tone for our work. Leah Doherty and Sally Trafton were continuing sources of encouragement and personal support. We also acknowledge the anonymous contributions of the hundreds of families who have shared their intimate experiences of health and illness with us over the years. We have tried to tell their stories in this volume.

CHAPTER

1

Families and Health: An Introduction

UNTIL RECENTLY, IT WAS POSSIBLE to study the traditional family social sciences for years without coming across the idea that families are composed of individuals who have bodies. Why has the biological dimension of family life been ignored by all but a few family scholars?

In the same vein, the medical sciences, concerned with the detection and treatment of human disease, have tended to sidestep the issue that sick people generally are part of a network of close relationships. Why has the family dimension of biological disease been ignored until recently by all but a few medical scientists?

The answers to these questions lie in the cultural and scientific heritage of the Western world. In the first half of the seventeenth century, René Descartes captured the fields of science and philosophy with this mechanical model of physics and biology. According to Descartes and the scientists who followed him, all of nature can be understood in the mechanical terms of matter and motion (Cohen, 1985). Although Descartes personally believed in the existence of a human spirit or "soul," he banished human thinking and feeling from the domain of science. The human body, from this viewpoint, is a machine that can be studied apart from its relationship with mind and social interactions. The human mind then becomes "a ghost in a machine."

A modern descendant of Descartes's philosophy is found in the biomedical model in medicine. As described by internist George Engel

(1977), the biomedical model eliminates psychological and social dimensions from the science and practice of medicine. All diseases are explained in biological terms only, for example, a virus or a wayward hormone. There is no need to resort to psychological and social explanations for why people get sick or regain health. The health care professional then becomes an applied biologist: scientifically assessing the biological issues and intervening with medication or surgery. In the biomedical model, the interpersonal aspects of health care remain in the background, outside the realm of science.

If modern medicine has had difficulty keeping the patient's mind and body together in a whole person, it should not be surprising that the family dimension of health and illness would remain obscure. What is remarkable is that the 1980s have witnessed widespread interest in family and health issues in a number of health care professions, in particular, family medicine, nursing, and social work (Doherty, 1985). The particulars of each professional group's interest in the family will be discussed later in this chapter.

Why are many health care professionals discovering or rediscovering the family? Although there is no clear-cut answer to this question, we believe that the following influences were involved. First, medical science, having conquered a number of major infectious diseases that killed people in their prime years, is now preoccupied with chronic diseases related to life-style and social environment. Smallpox and tuberculosis are examples of infectious diseases where the biomedical model appeared to be sufficient: find the virus or bacteria causing the disease, and then invent a vaccine or antibiotic to prevent or treat the disease. In 1910, about 60 of 100 deaths were caused by infectious processes, whereas now infectious disease accounts for only about 6 of 100 deaths (Glazier, 1973; Matarazzo, 1984). Heart disease and cancer, currently the leading killers, are examples of the "newer" diseases confronting the health sciences. A single cause is not likely to be found for either condition, and life-style factors such as diet and cigarette smoking are thought to be important contributors to these diseases.

The exclusively biological focus of medical science, then, has not proved sufficient to explain the more complex, chronic diseases that people get when they have survived or avoided the infectious diseases that used to end people's lives before the chronic diseases showed themselves. Nor is the biomedical model adequate to the challenge of helping individuals modify their life-styles in more healthful directions. Indeed, as the *Surgeon General's Report on Health Promotion and*

Disease Prevention attested, "Of the ten leading causes of death in the United States, at least seven could be substantially reduced if persons at risk improved just five habits: diet, smoking, lack of exercise, alcohol abuse, and use of antihypertensive medication" (Califano, 1979, p. 14).

If the causes of disease are beginning to be viewed in terms that allow for psychosocial factors, so too are treatment considerations. Even when treatment has been proven effective, many people fail to participate in it. A good example is high blood pressure or essential hypertension. Although the causes for this highly common and destructive disease are not known, effective treatment is available in the form of medications. Studies summarized by the National Heart, Lung, and Blood Institute (1982) have demonstrated, however, that the majority of diagnosed hypertensive individuals fail to take enough medication to control their blood pressure. The reasons for this widespread "noncompliance" (the term used by health professionals), and ways to change it, are currently the subjects of considerable research attention in contemporary health sciences. Twenty years ago, however, there was little research on this psychosocial cornerstone of health care delivery.

Once the leap was made from biology to life-style as an additional important factor in disease and treatment, the way was open to focus on the family dimensions of health and illness. Why? Once we talk about life-style, with its corresponding attitudes, beliefs, and habits, we are talking about families. As preventive medicine experts Tom Baranowski and Phillip Nader (1985) have pointed out, families are where health-related behaviors take form in childhood and are nurtured through adulthood. Take the example of cigarette smoking, probably the most widespread and deadly health behavior. Children are twice as likely to smoke if both parents smoke, twice as likely *not* to smoke if neither parent smokes, and in between when just one parent smokes (Nolte, Smith, & O'Rourke, 1983). Furthermore, if neither parent said he or she was upset about the child smoking, the child was five times more likely to smoke than if both parents said they were upset.

An additional factor leading to a new recognition of the importance of families in health care has come from societal concerns about the escalating costs of health care since the 1960s. Particularly burdensome are the costs of long-term care in institutions. Cost-containment issues coupled with the rapid growth of the elderly population, who are the group most likely to need long-term care, have stimulated clinicians, researchers, and government agencies to explore ways to support families in maintaining individuals at home during long-term care (Lave, 1985). The AIDS epidemic of the 1980s has also stimulated awareness of the human and economic benefits of caring for ill people at home.

THE BIOPSYCHOSOCIAL MODEL

Researchers in the health sciences, spurred by the practical considerations that interpersonal issues are important in health and illness, have taken inspiration in the biopsychosocial model of George Engel (1977). Engel proposed that a fully comprehensive and scientific model of medicine involves the simultaneous consideration of biological, psychological, and social issues. The biological factors must be understood as occurring in a human person who is an integrated mind-body organism. Body affects mind and mind affects body in such a way that neither notion makes sense alone. Furthermore, the human person exists within families and other social groups that provide the context for understanding the individual. The family affects the individual's health, and the individual's health affects the family. Similar dynamics occur in the family's relationship with larger social units such as the local community. Termed a "general systems" framework, Engel's biopsychosocial model explicitly rejects the one-cause/one-disease/one-treatment approach in favor of a comprehensive view of factors influencing health, illness, and health care.

This biopsychosocial model has inspired contemporary research on how psychosocial stress influences biological processes such as the immune system (Borysenko & Borysenko, 1982). Far from being a machine cut off from mental processes, the body involves complex connections between psychosocial experiences—such as reactions to bereavement and loss of employment—and changes in how the body produces cells that fight infection. (See Chapter 3 for a more detailed discussion.) Although the biomedical model still dominates medicine and shapes government support for research, scientific work stemming from the biopsychosocial model is gaining ground steadily (Doherty, Baird, & Becker, 1987).

The biopsychosocial model also implies a new kind of relationship between health care professionals and patients. The biomedical model fostered an authoritarian approach to patient care: The professional knows best and the patient's job is to follow orders. The biopsychosocial model, on the other hand, emphasizes the sharing of power among professional and patient and family. Health care transactions, especially in chronic conditions where life-style issues are so important, are best understood as ongoing exchanges of perspective and expertise among professionals, patients, families, and other important parties such as insurance providers. The "politics" of the biopsychosocial model, in fact, might turn out to be as revolutionary as its science (Doherty et al., 1987).

HEALTH CARE
PROFESSIONS AND THE FAMILY

At the same time that some leaders in health care were questioning the assumptions of the biomedical model, family therapy and family systems theory were beginning to make their mark in mental health care. Operating from the same general systems framework as Engel, family therapists during the 1960s and 1970s demonstrated new ways to understand the behavior and development of individuals within their family context. Similarly, the post-World War II period witnessed the flowering of family sociology in the United States. Particularly influential was the early work of family sociologist Reuben Hill (1949) on family stress. The convergence of these new understandings from family therapy and from family sociology caught the attention of three major health professions during the 1970s: family medicine, nursing, and social work. There had been isolated experiments in family-centered health care prior to 1960, but as psychologist and family therapist Donald Ransom (1981) points out, none of these captured the imagination of mainstream health professions until the family revival of the 1980s.

Family medicine was founded in 1969 as a replacement for general practice. Promoted actively by federal and state governments as an antidote to fragmented, impersonal medical care, family medicine from the beginning has aspired to a family perspective on health care. It thus became the first American medical specialty to endorse explicitly an emphasis on family and health issues. This idea, however, has been difficult to put into practice. It was only in the 1980s that a substantial literature base was created on the clinical aspects of family-centered medical care, and actual practice in family medicine lags behind this new literature. Chief examples are books by family physicians and family therapists such as Christie-Seely (1984), Doherty and Baird (1983, 1987), and Henao and Grose (1985). On the other hand, from the beginnings of family medicine, research on families and health has been perceived as an important area of inquiry, and, according to family physicians Larry Culpepper and Lorne Becker (1987), family medicine academic centers are beginning to produce meaningful research contributions in the family and health area.

Nursing historically has had an interest in the "whole patient" in the patient's social context (Newman, 1983). In addition, the field's long-term commitment to health promotion has led to a concern with the family dimensions of health and illness. This is particularly true for those nurses who have worked with patients in the home. Although nursing's underlying commitment to family issues has been present for a long time, only in the last decade, with the influence of family systems theory, has nursing begun explicitly to embrace a major emphasis on families. In 1984, the first text applying family systems theory to nursing practice was published by two nurse family therapists, Lorraine Wright and Maureen Leahey (1984). Family health nurses have taken leadership roles in the National Council on Family Relations, and they are continuing to define nursing's scientific and clinical missions in family health care (Gilliss, Highley, Roberts, & Martinson, in press).

Social work in health care has always defined its mission as dealing with the patient's social and environmental stressors. Social work lost its emphasis on families from the 1920s through the 1970s, however (Hartman & Laird, 1983). During that period, social workers tended to divide themselves between those who worked with individuals (usually from a psychoanalytic model) and those who worked with communities in organizational work. Only with the emergence in the 1970s of family systems theory and family therapy did social work recapture its emphasis on families in health care (Hartman & Laird, 1983).

Thus the 1980s have witnessed the flowering of interest in families in three powerful groups in the health care professions—family medicine, nursing, and social work. As Doherty (1985) has written elsewhere, this joint interest presents many possibilities for collaborative research and practice—and equally many possibilities of professional turf battles. The health of the family and health field will depend greatly on ability of these powerful professional groups to collaborate in pursuing new knowledge and better clinical practice.

THE SOCIAL/BEHAVIORAL
SCIENCES AND FAMILY HEALTH

Before health care professional groups discovered or rediscovered the family, sociologists and anthropologists were already generating an impressive amount of literature on families and health care (see the review by public health scholar Theodur Litman, 1974). This research centered on four major themes: families' access to health care, family as the group that defines illness, family support to sick members, and the impact of illness on the family. Important as this research was, generally it failed to capture the imagination of the health care professions. One reason may be that there was little work on the effect of family issues on the creation of clinical disease, and even less work on how taking a family perspective could aid in the prevention and treatment of disease in clinical settings. Stated differently, because the sociology and anthropology traditions have emphasized only the "psychosocial" part of the biopsychosocial model without integration with the "bio" part, and because these traditions have concentrated on *describing* family patterns rather than on *intervening*, their influence on clinical research and practice has been limited.

Family therapy and family systems theory have provided less research literature than the traditional social sciences, but more promise of clinical intervention. Furthermore, family therapists have worked more often in medical centers where clinical research and clinical experimentation take place. Two developments in the late 1970s foreshadowed an upsurge of interest in "family systems medicine" in the United States in the 1980s. First was family therapy pioneer John Weakland's paper on "family somatics" (Weakland, 1977). Second was the work of the Philadelphia Child Guidance Clinic team Salvador Minuchin, Bernice Rosman, and Lester Baker (1978), who found stress-related blood markers that differentiated parents of psychosomatically ill diabetic children from other ill children. Third, as more family therapists began to work in family medicine settings, more primary care physicians were trained in family therapy, and more nurses were trained in family systems theory, interest grew for a biopsychosocial perspective that blended biological and family systems information. This interest culminated in 1984 in the founding of the journal *Family Systems Medicine*. Thus, by the mid-1980s, family therapy had joined the attempt to bridge the mind-body dichotomy that has vexed the health care professions since Descartes.

An even more recent development has been the interest within American psychology in family dimensions of health and illness. Psychology's surging literature since the mid-1970s in the areas of health psychology and behavioral medicine has concentrated on individual behavior and interventions with individuals. In particular, psychologists have provided leadership in studying the influence of psychosocial stress on biological processes and disease (Jemmott & Locke, 1984), and factors associated with individual patient compliance with medical prescriptions (Dunbar & Stunkard, 1979). In general, health psychology in North America has been developing more of a *bio-psychological* model than a *bio-psycho-social* model. Recent activity, however, suggests that health psychology is broadening its scope to include family dimensions as well. In the first book published on families and health from the health psychology tradition, Dennis Turk and Robert Kerns (1985) write about their own evolution from individually focused health psychologists to a point where they added a family perspective. They speak for the experience of many professionals in this passage:

> In our own work on coping with chronic illness, we have experienced an increasing concern for the family, both for its role in the development and maintenance of health and illness behaviors and for its role in treatment and rehabilitation efforts. As our interest in the central role of families has increased, we have noted that others in a number of areas are coming to similar conclusions. (Turk & Kerns, 1985, p. xii)

Finally, we must say a word about psychiatry. A central birthplace of family therapy in the 1950s, psychiatry in the 1970s and 1980s has become more biomedical in its orientation. This is ironic at a time when other disciplines are becoming more comprehensive in orientation. Even in mainstream biological psychiatry, however, the 1980s have witnessed a growing consensus, based on well-controlled studies, that negative emotional interactions in families lead to relapse among schizophrenics. Furthermore, psychiatrist Ian Falloon and his colleagues (1984) have offered evidence that a combined family therapy-medication approach to the management of schizophrenics in the community is significantly more effective than the conventional treatment involving medication combined within individual psychotherapy.

Thus, even in a field that increasingly rejects the idea that family interactions can cause mental illness, certain family behavior patterns are beginning to be accepted as important in preventing the relapse of schizophrenic patients after they leave the hospital.

In sum, a number of forces seem to be coalescing around families and health. Several major health care professions have demonstrated new or renewed interest in families. Sociology and anthropology continue their historic interest, now supported by the potential of a wider interested audience. Health psychology shows early signs of discovering the family, and psychiatry is seeing families come in through the back door of the biomedical house.

FAMILY SCIENCE AND
FAMILY HEALTH

Family science is the new term being used to describe the interdisciplinary field of the family. Until the 1980s, family and health issues were not an important area of scholarly activity within family science. The prominent handbooks of family science, edited by sociologists, made little mention of health and illness issues (Burr, Hill, Nye, & Reiss, 1979; Christensen, 1964). There were, of course, exceptions, including the pioneering work of sociologists Marvin Sussman (1976) and Lois Pratt (1976). But, by and large, the physical health of family members did not receive prominent treatment in family science until family stress and coping researchers such as Hamilton McCubbin and Joan Patterson at the University of Minnesota began to apply their models to chronically and seriously ill individuals and their families (McCubbin et al., 1980; Patterson & McCubbin, 1983). This movement received a considerable boost when psychiatrists David Reiss and Peter Steinglass and their colleagues at George Washington University turned their attention to chronic illness in families (Reiss, Gonzalez, & Kramer, 1986). This development occurred in the context of greater openness among health professionals to allow family researchers access to clinical populations.

The early 1980s saw the birth of a "focus group" on families and health within the National Council on Family Relations, followed in 1984 by the creation of a standing section on families and health. In January 1985, the NCFR journal *Family Relations* published a special issue, "The Family and Health Care" (Doherty & McCubbin, 1985). Thus family science has moved quickly in the 1980s to develop its base in the health and illness aspects of family life. This development has been noted in particular by nursing researchers, who have begun an active dialogue with family scientists around family and health research (Murphy, 1986).

PURPOSE OF THIS VOLUME

This is the first book we are aware of that is intended as an introduction and overview of the family and health field for a multidisciplinary audience. Given that readers may range from undergraduate family science majors to practicing health care professionals and researchers, we have tried to do three things simultaneously: first, keep the writing nontechnical; second, demonstrate the principal ideas and findings in the field through discussing exemplar issues in some depth rather than trying to review the voluminous literature on families and health comprehensively; and third, blend research and theory presentations with case examples and implications for intervention. Our overall objective is to make the volume creative enough for experienced scholars in the field to benefit, but simple and interesting enough to reach persons with little background in the area. Although in the last chapter we will deal with important methodological issues in family and health research, the scope of this book does not allow detailed methodological critiques of individual studies.

Within the overall domain of health and illness, we chose to limit the emphasis of this book to illnesses commonly described as primarily "physical." (Of course, from a biopsychosocial viewpoint, all illnesses are both physical and psychosocial.) This decision was made mostly because the literature on the family factors in mental illness is far more extensive and widely known to students and family scholars than the family and physical illness literature is (Campbell, 1985). Furthermore, the renewed interest in family and health in the 1980s has concentrated on so-called physical illnesses that previously have been studied primarily from the perspective of the biomedical model and the individual psychological model. Because of these reasons and because of space limitations, we have not included in-depth discussions of important health problems such as alcoholism, depression, and schizophrenia.

When discussing clinical issues in family health, we have tried to keep in mind the range of health professionals who interact with families in the health care arena. Our emphasis, however, is on health professionals who deal with families on the "front line" of care, rather than on therapists and other specialized social service professionals who see families referred by primary care professionals. Because many clinical issues with families cut across professional disciplines, we frequently use the generic term *clinician* instead of a specific category such as physician, nurse, physician assistant, physical therapist, or nutritionist. We have attempted to use case illustrations from the work of a variety of health professionals. The reader should be aware, however, that our own experience has been primarily within family medicine settings. Professionals from other backgrounds may want to augment the clinical discussions in this volume with literature specific to their own field.

Finally, what do we mean by *family*? As students of the family know, there is no universally agreed upon definition of the family in the family sciences. The health field is no different. Indeed, the family can be thought to include long-deceased individuals who have passed certain genes on to the present generation, or only members of the household where a virus is being spread about. From a health care professional's viewpoint, the clinically relevant family varies according to the health problem: from a roommate to make chicken soup for a patient with a cold, to siblings and children all over the world when a decision is being made to institutionalize an elderly person or to turn off life-support systems for a dying person, to a same-sex lover who nurses a critically ill partner with AIDS. By and large, however, most of the research we will be reviewing in this volume has considered the family to be those people related to the ill person by blood, marriage, or adoption, who are significantly concerned with the health of the patient (Campbell, 1985).

The next section will describe the model used to organize this volume.

THE FAMILY HEALTH AND ILLNESS CYCLE

The academic literature in the family and health area has grown quite large and multifaceted. This was already the situation in 1974 when

Litman published his classic review of the family and health literature (Litman, 1974). By the mid-1980s, the literature had increased exponentially as the health professions and family researchers "discovered" family and health. Studies have been published on the family implications of a large number of diseases, on the impact of the family on the course of a large number of diseases, on families' utilization of health care, and on many other topics. The Family Health and Illness Cycle is an attempt to give some conceptual order to this vast literature. It was developed initially by William Doherty for a special issue of *Family Relations* (Doherty & McCubbin, 1985), and has been refined further for this volume.

The Family Health and Illness Cycle has two objectives: first, to organize the family and health literature into categories so that seemingly disparate areas of research can be seen as complementary; and, second, to suggest a temporal sequence of families' experience with health and illness. In addition, the two-way arrows between the family and the health care system represent the importance of the families' ongoing interactions with health care professionals and the wider health care system. This discussion will begin with an explanation of the categories and then move to the temporal aspects or phases of the model.

Figure 1.1 can be read best in clockwise fashion starting with "Family Health Promotion and Risk Reduction." This category refers to family beliefs and activities that help family members maintain good health through avoiding behaviors that increase their likelihood of becoming ill, and through engaging in activities that are believed to enhance personal health. The category can be thought of most easily as related to life-style issues. A balanced diet and regular exercise are examples of familial life-style patterns that are believed to promote the health and well-being of family members. Cigarette smoking is a prominent example of a behavior pattern that puts family members at risk for a wide range of diseases (National Center for Health Statistics, 1984).

Closely related to health promotion is the notion of risk reduction. The family is a principal focus of *risk reduction* activities when the behavior to be changed concerns longstanding life-style patterns learned in families and performed in families. The Council on Scientific Affairs of the American Medical Association (1983, p. 1877), in a statement symbolic of the new awareness of family influences on health behavior, made the following recommendation concerning interventions to reduce high blood cholesterol or hyperlipidemia:

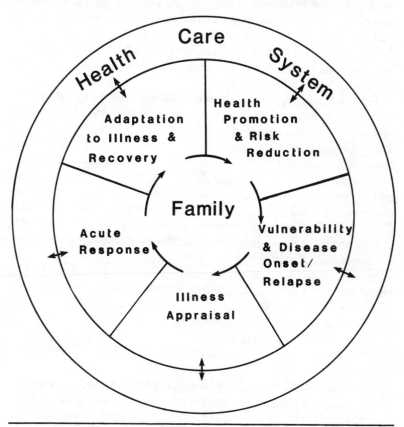

Figure 1.1 Family Health and Illness Cycle

One aid to reinforcement of the dietary program is family involvement. Because of the familial nature of many hyperlipidemias and because dietary management is a family affair, a good case can be made for extending dietary recommendations to the entire family of the patient.

In sum, "Family Health Promotion and Risk Reduction" refers to the wide range of activities whereby a family enhances healthful behaviors and avoids risky behaviors. Of course, the family does not engage in these activities in isolation from the health care system and the rest of society. Families are influenced by the health care professionals with whom they relate, by the media, and by the experiences of other families in their reference group. A new professional awareness of cancer risk, for example, may eventually permeate society enough to lead families to change their health beliefs and practices.

Chapter 2 in this book will discuss Family Health Promotion and Risk Reduction with reference to the leading cause of death in the United States: cardiovascular disease.

The next category, "Family Vulnerability and Disease Onset," refers to life events and experiences of the family that render family members susceptible to becoming ill or to having a relapse of a chronic illness. The principal idea here is that family stress related to internal or external conditions may predispose some family members to become ill. For example, the pediatrician Robert Haggerty and his colleagues found that bacterial throat infections in children were likely to be preceded by a stressful event in the family (Meyer & Haggerty, 1962). The New Zealand pediatric team of Beautrais, Fergusson, and Shannon (1982) reported that family stressful life events strongly predicted physician visits and hospitalizations.

In addition to the onset of new disease, this category also refers to relapsing from a chronic but controlled disease. An example is family factors predisposing a schizophrenic young adult to experience a relapse of his or her schizophrenia, as documented by the psychologist Jeri Doane and her colleagues (1985). Indeed, many chronic diseases such as diabetes and multiple sclerosis are characterized by a recurring course.

The exemplar topic we chose for the chapter on Family Vulnerability and Illness Onset/Relapse is bereavement, an experience that apparently leaves people more susceptible to the onset of disease.

"Family Illness Appraisal" refers to family beliefs about the illness of a family member and to family decisions about how to deal with the illness. There is a rich tradition of research in sociology and anthropology attesting to the family's role in verifying that an individual indeed is "sick," in explaining why the individual got sick, and in deciding whether the individual should seek professional attention or be cared for within the family or the family's lay network, an area studied by the physician/anthropologists Leon Eisenberg and Arthur Kleinman (1981).

In appraising the illness episode, the family gives its own meaning to the situation, a meaning that may be close to or distant from the professional consensus. Similarly, families differ widely in their utilization of health care services. The category of Family Illness Appraisal contains studies that examine why some families choose to send a member to a health care professional when other families treat the same problem at home (Gottlieb, 1976). Of course, these decisions are also affected by the availability and accessibility of health care to the family. Thus both family health beliefs and family decisions are made in interaction with the health care system, as indicated by the presence of the outside circle in Figure 1.1.

Family Illness Appraisal will be exemplified in Chapter 4 by a discussion of parents' decisions to seek medical attention for their children's symptoms.

"Families' Acute Response" refers to the immediate aftermath of illness for the family. This family experience is tied closely to family illness appraisal, inasmuch as the early response to an illness episode is heavily influenced by how serious the family believes it is and how adequate the treatment resources are perceived to be. The acute response phase concerns the immediate adjustments the family must make, say, for the hospitalization of a member with a heart attack. When the illness is disabling or life threatening, this is the time that Hill (1958) referred to as the "crisis" period after a powerfully stressful event: The family undergoes a period of disorganization when its normal coping patterns are not sufficient to handle the new demands. For less serious problems, the family's acute response may be limited to someone staying home from work to provide temporary caretaking activities for a sick member. For more serious problems, the family's acute response may involve assembling the whole extended family for extended vigils at the bedside of the ill member. In sum, the period after an illness onset and before the family restabilizes into an everyday pattern is described in this model as Family Acute Response.

The disease selected for exemplifying this category is the disease most dreaded by American families: cancer.

The final category in the Family Health and Illness Cycle is "Family Adaptation to Illness and Recovery." This refers to how the family reorganizes itself around a chronic illness or disability of a family member, and to the ways that a family adapts after the recovery of a family member. The family's sometimes difficult task is to promote the continued recovery or stabilization of the ill member while preserving the family's ability to nurture family members and to maintain its place in the community. In chronic illness, the family must also handle long-term, complex relationships with health care professionals and other societal agents such as insurance companies and governmental agencies. This process of adaptation has been the most extensively studied area in the family and health literature.

In Chapter 6 of this volume, diabetes will be discussed to exemplify the major issues related to family adaptation to illness and recovery.

We have found the Family Health and Illness Model to be a useful guide to placing the current research literature on family and health into meaningful categories. Beyond this clustering function, the model also presents a temporal sequence of families' experience with illness. Take the example of a heart attack stemming from coronary artery disease. The unfolding of this disease process in the family can be seen as occurring through a long health promotion and risk reduction phase influenced by family behaviors related to diet, exercise, and perhaps stress. The next, briefer phase—vulnerability and disease onset— occurs when there is a pileup of physical and psychosocial stressors that precipitate the heart attack in a family member, for example, shoveling a snowy sidewalk or arguing with a family member. The family then must evaluate the member's symptoms, decide whether to seek professional help, and evaluate the diagnosis and treatment plan of the health professionals. After this immediate family illness appraisal, and while continuing its appraisal process, the family begins to experience its acute response. This is likely to range from emotional reactions such as fear and shock, to behavioral reactions such as spending much time at the hospital or talking with extended family members and friends. The family is in its emergency mode of operating. Finally, the patient stabilizes after the heart attack, and returns home for rehabilitation. Here the family faces its adaptation to illness and recovery: At least temporarily, family roles must be renegotiated, and then the recovering member must either return to old roles or find new ones in the family. The cycle then can be seen as beginning anew as the family deals with reducing the risk of a repeated heart attack in the health promotion and risk reduction phase. Chapter 7 will discuss in more detail the family's experience of coronary heart disease over the full cycle.

The Family Health and Illness Cycle, then, can help us capture the family's experience with an illness over time. This temporal pattern might be useful to clinicians and researchers in the following way. Because most studies examine families at a particular point in time, typically during the adaptation to illness and recovery phase, researchers and clinicians seeking to understand the family's current functioning around the illness may profit from learning about how the family handled earlier phases. The family of a cancer patient, for example, may have cut off sources of social support during the acute phase, or have developed a catastrophic appraisal of the disease prognosis, based perhaps on the family's previous experiences with cancer. The Family Health and Illness Cycle, then, can be used to guide the clinician or researcher to probe past family experiences with this illness or related ones, thereby shedding light on the family's current experience.

Because of the focus on a family's experience with a particular illness, however, this framework does not capture the complex dynamics involved in multiple illnesses in family members. A family, for example, might be in the adjustment phase with father's heart disease and the illness appraisal phase with mother's newly diagnosed rheumatoid arthritis. Nor does the model show all the important interactions between the family and other social groups. Individual psychological dynamics likewise are not examined. Nor is the family's level of general functioning—for example, its cohesion and adaptability (Olson, 1986) or its general problem-solving paradigm (Reiss, 1981). These dimensions of family life presumably influence how a family negotiates its journey through the phases of the Family Health and Illness cycle. Finally, in carving up the "pie" of family experiences with health, the model separates into time blocks family processes that may occur simultaneously in some situations. For example, in emergencies, the family may be said to experience a strong acute response (e.g., fear, panic) at the same time that it is appraising the symptoms. The Family Health and Illness Cycle, then, is intended to shed light selectively on certain important aspects of families' experience with illness, while inevitably leaving in the shadows other important issues. This assertion of the framework's limitations is not an apology: A fully comprehensive model at this stage of our knowledge would be unwieldy and probably misleading.

Finally, the cycle as depicted in Figure 1.1 is intended to reflect the pervasive interaction of the family with the health care system. At each phase of the cycle, as represented by the arrows, the family is influenced by health professionals working clinically and in the media and societal institutions. From birth to death, the family cannot make certain major decisions without reference to the expectations of health professionals who represent the larger society. Examples are vaccinations, school physicals, quarantining, giving birth, and the care of dying family members. In less direct ways, families in contemporary North

America are instructed continually by health professionals in the media about health and disease. Moreover, health professionals tend to focus on different dimensions of the family health and illness cycle, with physicians traditionally tending to emphasize the vulnerability and acute response phases (family medicine is attempting to expand this limited scope) and nurses tending to emphasize the health promotion, illness appraisal, and adaptation phases. Overspecialization of health professionals can lead to discontinuity of services for families throughout the course of a long illness.

The arrow of influence also goes from families to the health care system. Families of patients with common disabling diseases such as Alzheimer's disease and cystic fibrosis have banded together to promote research and to insist on optimal care for their family members from the health care system. Families are reaching out to other families through these self-help groups, sometimes bypassing the health care system when it is deemed unresponsive. An even more far-reaching illustration of family influence is the widespread allowing of family members to be involved in the birthing process; this development was initiated by families, not by obstetricians. In the consumer-driven health care marketplace of the 1980s, families have increased opportunities to influence their own health care.

Another circle could be added to Figure 1.1, representing the rest of society, which interacts with the health care system in numerous ways. Many scholars, such as the sociologist Paul Starr (1982), believe that the dramatic changes in the health care system during the 1980s—such as the rise of prepaid systems like HMOs, and the increase of corporate ownership of health care facilities—have been a response by the larger society to the excesses of the health care system. In order to make the scope and size of this book manageable, we will not deal extensively with these societal aspects of family health. Our focus will be on how families experience illness and relate to health care professionals. We will, however, remind readers from time to time that larger social forces are involved in every family's experience with health, illness, and health care.

DISCUSSION QUESTIONS

(1) Do you agree that there has been a mind-body split in Western culture? Is this reflected in the organization of modern science? How do you explain this phenomenon?

(2) If health care professionals began to take the family seriously in health care, how might they act differently in caring for patients?

(3) Take a disease that you are acquainted with from your family experience, and trace its development through the family health and illness cycle.

RECOMMENDED READINGS

Doherty, W. J., & McCubbin, H. I. (Eds.). (1985). The family and health care [Special issue]. *Family Relations, 34,* 1.

Turk, D. C., & Kerns, R. D. (Eds.). (1985). *Health, illness, and families: A lifespan perspective.* New York: John Wiley.

Wright, L. M., & Leahey, M. (1984). *Nurses and families.* Philadelphia: F. A. Davis.

CHAPTER

2

Family Health Promotion and Risk Reduction

We are killing ourselves with our own careless habits.

Joseph Califano
Secretary of the U.S. Department of
Health, Education and Welfare (1979)

WE HAVE MADE CONSIDERABLE PROGRESS toward defeating the external enemies to good health and a long life. The great plagues that killed millions, the stray bacteria that invaded a wound and ravaged the body of a man or woman in the prime of life, have been successfully subdued in modern America by vaccinations, improved sanitation, and antibiotics. Ironically, our own behavior is now the principal source of illness and premature death. Two life-style-related diseases, cardiovascular disease and cancer, currently account for 75% of all deaths in the United States. Overall, the federal government has estimated that half of U.S. mortality is due to unhealthful life-styles (U.S. Department of Health, Education, and Welfare [DHEW], 1978).

Calling for a "second revolution in health care," the 1979 U.S. *Healthy People: The Surgeon General's Report on Health Promotion and Disease Prevention* (Califano, 1979) recommended a major commitment to prevent premature mortality and morbidity (disease).

The report concluded that six life-style changes would substantially reduce the numbers of premature deaths each year: (a) elimination of cigarette smoking; (b) reduction of alcohol misuse; (c) moderate dietary changes to reduce intake of excess calories, fat, salt, and sugar; (d) moderate exercise; (e) periodic screening (at intervals determined by age and sex) for major disorders such as high blood pressure and certain cancers; and (f) adherence to speed laws and use of seat belts.

This chapter will review the empirical evidence for the influence of the family on the prevention of cardiovascular or heart disease, the number one cause of death in the United States. In addition, we will discuss the interaction between health care professionals, patients, and their families around life-style issues. Finally, we will offer implications for clinicians and recommendations for the care of patients and their families in the area of health promotion and risk reduction.

FAMILY INFLUENCE ON
CARDIOVASCULAR RISK

Because cardiovascular disease frequently strikes middle-aged men and women in their most productive years, it has a major impact on society as a whole. It has been estimated that approximately 50% of heart disease is due to the life-style factors of smoking, diet, and lack of exercise (Dever, 1980). Since the 1960s, a major public health campaign has been directed against cardiac risk factors, resulting in a dramatic drop in incidence of heart attacks and cardiac-related deaths (Califano, 1979).

The major risk factors for cardiovascular disease are excess cholesterol in the blood (hypercholesterolemia), cigarette smoking, obesity, lack of exercise, hypertension, diabetes, and a family history of heart disease. All but the last can be altered by life-style changes. Changes in diet can lower cholesterol levels and reduce weight. Most cases of adult-onset diabetes result from relative insulin resistance caused by obesity and can be treated by weight reduction. Weight loss and salt restriction can lower blood pressure. Control of even mild hypertension results in fewer heart attacks and strokes. Smoking cessation dramatically reduces the risk of heart disease. Moderate exercise (20 minutes, three times a week) is associated with significantly lower heart disease and longer life span overall.

Despite the overwhelming evidence for the benefits of cardiovascular risk reduction, these behavioral risk factors remain highly prevalent in American society (Califano, 1979). According to the 1985 Health Promotion and Disease Prevention Survey conducted by the National Center for Health Statistics (1986), three in ten American adults smoke cigarettes, despite a high understanding of the risks. Less than half of the adult population exercises on a regular basis. These habits become entrenched in our life-styles and are often very difficult for individuals to change. The next sections document the family dimensions of these high-risk behaviors.

Concordance of Risk Factors Within Families

Numerous studies, such as one conducted by preventive medicine researcher Thomas Baranowski and colleagues (1982), have documented a high concordance of the cardiovascular risks within families, that is, family members are more likely to share the same risk factors, than would be expected by chance. This is particularly true for smoking, obesity, hypercholesterolemia, and hypertension, and occurs both between spouses and among parents and children. The famous Framingham study on the development of heart disease, for example, found a higher than expected concordance between spouses for blood pressure, cholesterol, triglyceride, blood sugar, smoking, and lung function (Sackett et al., 1975). It appears that family members share risks for heart disease along with their hearth and home.

There are several explanations for these findings. The most important is that family members influence each other's health habits. Families usually eat a similar diet and, therefore, similar amounts or proportions of salt, saturated fats, cholesterol, and perhaps calories. Adolescents are much more likely to smoke if either of their parents smokes (Bewley & Bland, 1977). The emphasis on physical fitness and maintaining ideal body weight is often a shared family value.

Genetics may also play a role in many of these risk factors, leading to similarities among parents and children. In a recent study of obesity in adopted children, psychiatrist Albert Stunkard and his coinvestigators (1986) concluded that obesity in children is largely determined by genetics. Other studies have demonstrated that the familial environment has a significant effect (Garn et al., 1976; Hartz et al., 1977). One study of twins demonstrated that most of the concordance of cholesterol levels is due to environmental effects, primarily similar diets (Feinleib et al., 1977).

Another explanation for similarities in risk factors between *spouses* is that they may have had these characteristics prior to marriage. Obese men tend to marry obese women. Smokers tend to marry other smokers. Marital partners may even chose each other (consciously or unconsciously) based upon their dietary habits. On this point, the Framingham study did not find any *increase* in concordance of risk factors between spouses over time, which suggests that these similarities existed at the time of marriage (Sackett et al., 1975).

Whatever the causes of this phenomenon of family concordance for health risks, it has major implications for health care providers. If one member of a family has a particular cardiovascular risk factor, other family members are likely to have it as well. An intervention designed to change the risk factors within the *family* rather than in only one individual may be more efficient and cost effective. Of course, a behavior may also be more difficult to change if it is shared by several members of the family. Smokers are less likely to stop smoking if someone else in the family is a smoker (Price et al., 1981). Finally, if the family's life-style is tied up in the risk factor, then changing one member's risk behavior may have a ripple effect through the family. Responses may range from undermining the change to embracing it for the whole family, as when one family member starts an exercise program and other family members join in.

Cigarette Smoking

Smoking results in the greatest number of preventable deaths in the United States. Smokers are three times more likely to suffer a heart attack than nonsmokers. They have an increased risk of stroke, chronic lung disease, and cancer from multiple sites including lung, oral cavity, esophagus, stomach, pancreas, bowel, and bladder (Fielding, 1985). Smoking is also detrimental to nonsmokers within the family. The fetus of a pregnant smoker is at risk for low birth weight and prematurity. Children of smokers suffer an increased number of acute respiratory infections and chronic lung problems. Studies of passive exposure to cigarette smoke among adults are still controversial, but suggest an increased risk of cancer (Weiss et al., 1983).

Unfortunately, smoking is a difficult habit or addiction to quit. Although 80% of smokers report that they would like to stop, only a small proportion succeed (Fielding, 1985). In the best smoking intervention studies with highly motivated smokers, the abstinence rates at one year are between 20% and 40%. Most programs have emphasized smoking as an individual habit and conceptualize it as a maladaptive response to stress. Until recently, little attention has been paid to the social context of smoking, how it is influenced by family and friends, and what role it plays in relationships.

We know that smokers tend to be married to other smokers (Sutton, 1980), and to smoke a similar number of cigarettes per day as their partners (Venters et al., 1984). An adolescent is most likely to smoke if the same-sex parent smokes (Bewley & Bland, 1977; U.S. DHEW, 1976). Smoking couples tend to quit smoking at the same time (Venters et al., 1984). Smokers are more likely to quit if they are married to nonsmokers (Price et al., 1981), and to remain abstinent longer if their spouses or friends do not smoke (Lichtenstein, 1982; Ockene et al., 1981). Several studies have demonstrated that support from the spouse is associated with successful quitting (Graham & Gibson, 1971; Ockene et al., 1982). The psychologist Robin Mermelstein and her colleagues (1983) found that the smoker's partner's cooperation and reinforcement of a smoking cessation program correlated with a lower relapse rate, while "nagging" and "policing" by the partner had the opposite effect. Further work by the psychologists H. Catherina Coppotelli and C. Tracy Orleans (1985) demonstrated that the following specific behaviors of the smoker's partner predicted successful quitting: offering general problem-solving assistance and specific help with cravings or cigarette substitutes; rewarding quitting; and understanding, listening, and facilitating the enactment of coping and nonsmoking skills.

Using a family systems perspective, William Doherty and D'Ann Whitehead (1986) have examined the family dynamics of cigarette smoking. They view smoking as a form of communication within relationships that can be used to make statements about *inclusion* (being together or alone, being similar or different), *control* (who is in charge of whose smoking), and *intimacy* (personal closeness and sexual behavior) in the relationship. They suggest that attempts to quit smoking may result in changes in these interactional patterns, sometimes leading to undermining and relapse that restore the previous balance of the relationship. Similarly, some smokers may not feel "free" to quit smoking because this would be experienced as tantamount to a surrender to the partner who has been promoting the quitting effort.

Nutrition

Three components of diet are directly related to the risk of cardiovascular disease. Hypercholesterolemia results in part from the excess ingestion of cholesterol and saturated (animal) fats. The American Heart Association has recommended that all middle-aged adults consume a low-cholesterol diet (American Heart Association, 1984). Hypertension appears to be related to the high salt content in the diet. Excess total calorie consumption results in obesity, which is associated with elevated cholesterol, and is an independent risk factor for hypertension and cardiovascular disease.

Extensive research has been done on the role of obesity within families, and the interaction between family dynamics and obesity. Studies by psychologists such as Oscar Barbarin and Mildred Tirado (1984) suggest that eating behavior and obesity itself play an important homeostatic function within many families. In a survey of eating behavior within families, 25% of mothers reported that they used food as a reward for their children, and 10% used it as punishment (Bryan & Lowenberg, 1958). In one weight reduction program, 91% of the spouses of the obese women reported that they wished their wives would lose weight, but only 49% were willing to help (Stuart & Davis, 1972). About half of these men anticipated that weight loss would have an adverse effect on the marriage due to loss of eating as a shared activity, loss of power in marital conflicts, and concern over marital commitment and sexual fidelity. During recorded mealtime conversations, the husbands were seven times more likely to talk about food than their dieting wives, and four times more likely to offer food to the other. The men criticized their dieting wives twelve times more often than they praised them.

The family can have a significant effect on the treatment of obesity. Four randomized controlled trials have examined the impact of spouse or partner involvement in weight reduction programs (Brownell et al., 1978; Pearce et al., 1981; Saccone & Israel, 1978; Wilson & Brownell, 1978). All but one of these studies (Wilson & Brownell, 1978) demonstrated positive results. These studies have used a behavioral paradigm in which family members provide immediate and long-term reinforcement for weight loss or dieting. Overall, these studies have shown that groups with spouse involvement lose more weight and maintain the weight loss. In one study (Pearce et al., 1981), women whose husbands were told not to interfere with the weight loss program lost nearly as much weight as those whose husbands were trained in monitoring and reinforcing techniques, suggesting that one effect of involving the spouse is to prevent interference with or sabotage of the program.

One cannot assume that family involvement in a treatment program will always be advantageous. In a treatment trial of obese adolescents, the behavioral psychologist Kelly Brownell and his colleagues (1983) at the University of Pennsylvania demonstrated an adverse effect of the mothers' participation. At the one-year follow-up after an intensive weight reduction program, neither the obese adolescents whose mothers were actively involved in the program, nor the ones whose mothers were not involved, lost any weight. Only in the group in which the mothers were involved in their own separate and concurrent group did the adolescents lose weight. Understanding the life cycle tasks of the adolescent (especially the need for individuation) and the family dynamics of some obese patients (mother's overinvolvement in the child's life, including eating) can explain why a mother's active involvement with the daughter might be harmful. One might expect similar results of the family involvement in any adolescent's treatment that did not also respect the adolescent's need for independence.

The treatment of obesity can have either a positive or an adverse effect on families. The spouses of 12 women undergoing surgical treatment of obesity (intestinal bypass) reported increased anxiety and depression after surgery, which led to marital strife, increased impotence in the husbands, and extramarital affairs in the wives (Marshall & Neill, 1977). Only two of the twelve spouses were pleased with the increased sexual drive of the patients. The authors hypothesized that the obesity played an important protective function in the family: protecting against sexual demands, competition with others of the same sex, fears of abandonment, and marital conflicts. Other studies, however, have found mainly positive reports by spouses of changes in the marriage after this bypass surgery (Dano & Hahn-Pedersen, 1977; Rand et al., 1982; Solow & Silberfarb, 1974).

The role of the family in other aspects of diet and nutrition has not been well studied. In the only published study of the family and hypercholesterolemia, Doherty and colleagues (1983) examined the role of the spouse's health beliefs and support on the compliance of a group of men in a cholesterol-lowering program. The wife's beliefs regarding how susceptible she thought her husband was to harmful effects of elevated cholesterol were correlated to her support for her husband's compliance with taking a cholesterol-lowering drug. The wife's support in turn correlated with the husband's documented drug-taking behavior. Specifically, the wife's "interest in the program" and "reminding him about medicine or diet" correlated with compliance, while "nagging about medicine" was correlated with lower compliance. The delicate balance between "reminding" and "nagging" seems to tip the scales between positive support and negative undermining in the areas of medication taking and life-style change.

Hypertension

Hypertension, or high blood pressure, is a common cardiovascular risk factor that is easy to identify and relatively easy to treat. Studies have demonstrated that adequate treatment of elevated blood pressure significantly lowers the risk of heart attacks and strokes. Unfortunately, a number of research studies have estimated that only one-fourth of all hypertensive individuals are under treatment and only one-half of those under treatment have their blood pressure adequately controlled (McKenney et al., 1973). Compliance with medication is a major problem in the treatment of hypertension and reduction of cardiovascular disease.

A major intervention study by public health scholar Donald Morisky and colleagues (1983) at Johns Hopkins demonstrated a dramatic effect of family involvement on hypertension compliance and overall mortality. The study compared three different educational interventions (brief individual counseling, instructing the spouse or significant other during a home visit, and patient group sessions) in improving appointment keeping, weight control, and medication compliance. Involving the spouse not only improved overall compliance, but resulted in a significant lowering of blood pressure and overall mortality. While all the experimental groups had a significant effect, with a 57% overall reduction in mortality, the groups that included education of the spouse tended to do the best. The family intervention in this study was included after 70% of the clinic's hypertensive patients indicated on a survey that they wished that family members knew more about hypertension (Levine et al., 1979). A similar study by health educator Jo Anne Earp and colleagues (1982) failed to demonstrate any additional benefit of involving family members during a home visit, but the patients may not have been followed long enough to detect an effect.

The increased evidence for the importance of the family in the control of hypertension and heart disease has not escaped the notice of national leaders in health care. Based upon studies of the role of social supports in improving compliance, the National Heart, Lung, and Blood Institute has stressed the importance of "the help that patients receive from their family and friends to carry on with their treatments" (Haynes et al., 1982).

Multiple Cardiovascular Risk Factors

Thus far we have dealt with risk factors separately. The combination of several risk factors, however, is the most potent predictor of heart disease. Several studies of multiple risk factor reduction have examined the role of family members. Behavioral scientists Fred Heinzelman and Richard Bagley (1970) surveyed a group of men with multiple cardiac risk factors who were enrolled in an exercise program. While the men did not think that their wives influenced their decision to join the program, those men whose wives had positive attitudes about the program were twice as likely to complete the program than those men who had wives who were neutral or negative. Family therapist Fred Hoebel (1976) treated "difficult cardiac patients" who would not change their high-risk cardiac behaviors, by working only with their wives. In three to five sessions, he showed the women how their own behaviors were maintaining the high-risk behaviors of their spouses, and what they could do to modify those behaviors. In seven of the nine cases, there was a significant improvement in the high-risk behaviors. In a randomized controlled trial, Baranowski et al. (1982) showed the effectiveness of multifamily groups for increasing families' support for dietary and exercise changes.

In summary, there is strong evidence for both healthy and unhealthy influences by families on cardiovascular risk factors. Several controlled trials have demonstrated that family involvement improves the results of weight reduction and one study shows a similar result for hypertension control. Similar studies are needed for exercise programs, smoking cessation, and dietary changes (lowering salt and cholesterol). Despite the evidence for efficacy of a family approach to prevention, most health care providers tend to remain focused on the individual. Their training has not prepared them adequately for understanding and engaging families in clinical practice. The next section deals with the challenges that arise when clinicians and families work toward the goals of promoting health and preventing disease.

HOW PROFESSIONALS AND
FAMILIES INTERACT AROUND
RISK REDUCTION

Despite the rise of systems theory and the biopsychosocial model, the more narrow biomedical approach remains dominant in health care today. Most health care professionals, especially physicians, are trained in hospitals where the latest technology is used to treat acute life-threatening illnesses, and little attention is paid to psychological or social factors (Engel, 1977). As a result, clinicians tend to assume an action-oriented, authoritarian role toward patients and their problems. Physicians in particular are most comfortable when they can "do" something for the patient (e.g., perform an operation, prescribe a medication, or admit to the hospital). While this approach is quite successful for many acute illnesses, it commonly leads to failure when applied to chronic illnesses and health promotion.

Health risk behaviors rarely have a specific cause or a simple solution. Patients with risk factors often do not have symptoms and may not want any treatment. The behaviors are usually an integral part of a patient's life, and often serve an important function. When the clinician attempts to take control of a patient's risk factors and apply a strictly biomedical solution to them, problems arise. For example, many physicians are more likely to prescribe a cholesterol lowering drug than to help patients change their diets (even though the efficacy of most of these drugs remains unproven, and the side effects are significant). Coronary artery bypass grafts, one of the most common operations currently performed in the United States, are often performed without attempting to reduce cardiac risk factors. Unfortunately, the artery clogging process (arteriosclerosis) continues in the grafts. Bypassing an artery has become the high-tech solution to a problem that for many people is behavioral in origin.

Clinicians' Health Beliefs

Several health beliefs commonly held by physicians and other health professionals appear to interfere with their ability to work cooperatively with patients and families in promoting health and reducing risks. Most clinicians, believing that health should be patients' highest priority, have difficulty understanding why patients prefer to continue enjoyable behaviors that are harmful to their health. They also tend to believe that health activities are largely under cognitive control, and that, given accurate information, individuals will choose the healthiest behavior. Therefore, attempts to change risk factors are often limited to education, and patients who don't change receive more and more health instruction until the clinician gives up in frustration. Thus noncompliant hypertensives or obese diabetics are repeatedly lectured about the importance of taking medication or sticking to a diet, and warned of the potential consequences of their behaviors. The lack of success of this popular clinical approach is well documented in the research literature (Haynes, Taylor, & Sackett, 1979), and legendary in clinical experience.

Some health care professionals, believing that life-style changes are relatively easy to make, prescribe them as they would a simple medication. A nutritionist may prescribe a low-cholesterol diet ("Eat no more than one egg and two servings of red meet per week"), or a cardiac rehabilitation nurse may recommend an exercise program ("Exercise three times per week for 20 minutes"). Numerous studies have demonstrated that compliance even with simple short-term medication regimens is often poor, and that the longer a medication must be taken and the more complex the treatment regimen (number of drugs, variety of dosage schedules), the less likely the patient is to follow it (Haynes et al., 1979). Helping people change their life-style is even more difficult, because it requires an understanding of the *context* of the patient's life—the psychological, familial, and cultural dynamics in which life-style activities are embedded.

Power and the
Responsibility for Change

When health professionals attempt to apply a biomedical solution to health risk reduction, they often get caught in a power struggle over who is responsible for change (Ross & Phipps, 1986). The clinician may become overresponsible when attempting to "take charge" or assume responsibility for changing the patient's behavior, over which neither the clinician nor the family has any direct control. Typically, the provider tries to convince the patient to change—to lose weight, stop smoking, or take hypertension medication faithfully—without asking whether he or she really wants to make these changes. In some cases, patients want to change and do so. Many patients, however, are ambivalent or resistant to the recommended changes. They are aware of the difficulties and sacrifices of changing. They may resent the clinicians attempts to make them give up cherished personal habits such as smoking or eating salty foods. They may not want to be forced to follow "doctor's orders" for the rest of their lives. Ironically, for some patients, noncompliance—not cooperating with the clinician's orders—may be one way of keeping personal control over their health problems (Conrad, 1985).

Efforts by the clinician to push the patient into changing unhealthy habits may make the situation worse. The patient may become *under*responsible and further resist any changes, setting up a struggle for control. The more the provider pressures the patient, the more resistant the patient becomes, and the provider may get increasingly annoyed. The struggle can assume a life of its own and become the primary focus of their interactions. The provider becomes the pursuer and the patient a distancer (Fogarty, 1979). Each visit begins with "How much are you smoking?" or "Have you lost any weight since last visit?" Eventually, the provider may become so frustrated by the non-compliance, that he or she "gives up" and in turn becomes under-responsible. This can be done explicitly by excluding the patient from the clinical practice ("There is no sense in my caring for you if you won't listen to any of my advice"), or implicitly by blaming the patient, getting angry, or scheduling appointments farther and farther apart.

CASE ILLUSTRATION

Mrs. B., a 58-year-old obese woman with adult-onset diabetes, was referred to a nutritionist for weight reduction. After obtaining a detailed dietary history, the nutritionist prescribed a 1400-calorie American Diabetic Association diet and instructed Mrs. B. to return biweekly to review the diet and be weighed. Each visit, the nutritionist reviewed Mrs. B.'s food diary and made further suggestions to reduce calories. Because Mrs. B. failed to lose weight, however, the diet was changed to 1200 calories and visits were made weekly. Despite trying this more intensive program for four months, Mrs. B. did not lose any weight. In frustration, the nutritionist sent Mrs. B. back to her physician explaining that she could not lose weight on a diet and should consider intestinal bypass surgery.

After repeated interactions with "resistant" or noncompliant patients such as Mrs. B., the provider may take a very fatalistic and underresponsible position with all patients who have major health risks. Such clinicians assume that most people cannot change these behaviors, and that their responsibility is merely to provide the "medical" information to the patients and let patients decide whether to change ("It's up to you!"). When most of these patients do not change with this approach, the clinician's pessimism is reinforced. The most obvious example of this approach is the treatment of alcoholism. Despite the clear evidence that alcoholism is treatable, clinicians are very pessimistic about their ability to help alcoholics. It is commonly said that the alcoholic must "hit bottom" and decide on his or her own to stop drinking, and that other interventions are ineffectual. Clinicians here reflect the larger American society, which, in our view, has tended to take an underresponsible stance regarding alcoholism by ignoring the seriousness of the problem, not providing adequate treatment programs, and limiting access to existing programs.

Although the health professional can make a significant impact on life-style modification, most of these changes occur within the family, without the assistance or even recommendation of a health profes- sional. Television and newspapers are filled with information about the risks of smoking and high-cholesterol diets and the benefits of regular exercise. An individual may decide to attempt to make some life-style modifications and then request the family's assistance, or the family may believe that one family member needs to alter a health risk factor and try to get the individual to make the change.

Families can have a negative as well as a positive influence on compliance with health risk reduction (Strickland et al., 1981). The pattern of over- and underresponsibility for health problems can be seen within families and may mirror the patient-health care provider interaction. The family may be aware of a health risk in one of its members and believe that it is their responsibility to change the behavior. For example, the family of a patient with lung disease may believe that they can save the patient's life by getting him or her to stop smoking. They may start hiding cigarettes, removing ashtrays, and nagging the patient about smoking. The patient may respond by becoming angry and being more resistant to changing. As pointed out by the family therapists John Weakland and Richard Fisch (1984) from the Mental Research Institute, the family's well-intentioned attempts to help the patient can actually result in making the problem worse.

William Doherty and the family physician Macaran Baird (1983) have described a therapeutic triangle in health care consisting of the relationships among the health care provider, the patient, and the family. In any three-member system, two members of the triangle may join against the third in a coalition. For example, if a public health nurse feels responsible for getting a homebound man with chronic lung disease to quit smoking, the nurse may form a coalition with the family by encouraging them to hide his cigarettes and report his smoking to his physician. This may backfire, of course, when the family considers the nurse's efforts intrusive and joins with the patient against the nurse. As for the third possibility in the triangle, the nurse may join with the patient in viewing the family's efforts as "interfering," and then try to exclude them from the patient's care. The difficult task for the provider is to support the patient's legitimate autonomy concerning personal health, while maintaining a good working alliance with the family. Coalitions that exclude either the patient or the family undermine the long-term success of the clinician's efforts to promote better health.

IMPLEMENTING A FAMILY APPROACH TO HEALTH PROMOTION AND RISK REDUCTION

A family approach to health promotion and risk reduction requires a shift from the biomedical to a biopsychosocial or systems approach to health care (Engel, 1977). Medications or surgery are rarely the solution to life-style changes, and the limitations of the biomedical approach need to be acknowledged. Health care professionals must consider the context of the health risk behaviors and examine the physiological, psychological, and social influences upon these behaviors. This broader approach starts with the recognition that individuals are members of families, and that families have a major influence on health-related behaviors.

Using the contextual approach of the biopsychosocial model helps the clinician appreciate the difficulties of changing life-styles, and the patience required in helping people change. Personal and familial habits established over many years rarely change overnight. This can be difficult to accept for health professionals who were trained in acute care hospitals where changes occur over minutes and hours. Instead, this approach requires the type of ongoing relationships with patients that occur in primary care, the front line of outpatient health care delivery. Here clinicians learn to work for small changes and to expect the setbacks and failures that are an inevitable part of change.

The biopsychosocial approach also involves a different style of working with patients and their families, namely, a less authoritarian and more cooperative approach. The goal is to assist the patient and family to make the life-style changes that they want to make and agree to make. This goal avoids trying to coerce the patients and families into changing, or expecting them to change all on their own.

Family Assessment

Given that the most important social influence on health promotion and risk reduction is the family, family-oriented health professionals should be skillful in assessing families and their influences upon health behaviors. An understanding of the family dynamics surrounding the health risk behavior will assist the clinician in formulating interventions and avoid attempting unsuccessful strategies that the family has tried.

Family assessment is most easily accomplished by assembling the entire family. Interviewing the family, the clinician can explore both the family factors that may influence the present unhealthy behavior and the recommended changes. The following factors should be considered:

(1) Family stress. What is the level of stress in the family and how will it affect the family's ability to assist the patient? Families under a great deal of stress may be unable to make any changes or may not have the resources to promote health. Have there been any recent major life events in the family, such as deaths, major illnesses, marital discord, or financial crises? Unresolved grief reactions, for example, are common in families of substance abusers. How well are the stressors being dealt with? Mental or physical illness in other family members may be a sign of the family's difficulty in coping with stress. Parenthetically, the clinician may advise against initiating stressful life-style changes such as dieting and smoking cessation at a time when the family is already under enormous stress. Failed attempts at this time may add to the individual's feeling of hopelessness.

(2) Family health beliefs. What are the family's beliefs about this particular behavior, the recommended changes, and the disease to be prevented? Do the individual's beliefs conflict with the family's? Interventions should be adapted or framed in such a way that they are acceptable to the family and "fit" with their beliefs. Is there a family "health expert" (often the eldest female) or a health professional in the

family? The advice of these family members should be sought, and their expertise acknowledged.

(3) The role of the behavior in the family. Who is likely to be most affected by a change in the unhealthy behavior? Is the behavior used as a means of communication (e.g., smoking), a sign of loyalty (e.g., obese child of an obese parent), or a way of establishing autonomy (e.g., experimenting with drugs)?

(4) Family's response to recommendations. Who agrees/disagrees that the patient should change? Who feels most responsible for bringing about change? How will the recommended changes affect other family members, and how will they react? For instance, if a new diet is recommended, the food preparer may not be willing to change the menu. If other family members share the same habit or risk factor, are they interested in changing as well?

Before discussing any life-style modification, the clinician should encourage patients to identify the risk factor that they are most interested in working on. In dealing with patients who have multiple cardiac risk factors, health professionals often recommend altering the risk factors that they are most interested in, or that they believe to be the most serious, without considering what the patient wants to work on. In general, only one risk factor should be dealt with at a time. Attempting to make several changes (e.g., giving up smoking and changing diet) at once is more likely to lead to failure and disappointment. Once an agreement is made with the patient about the target of change, a family conference should be called.

The clinician's goal during the family session is to elicit family members' perspectives on the problem and to establish the support of the family for the final recommendations. One effective method for accomplishing this goal is to have the patient set up a behavioral contract with the family for what assistance the family is willing to give and what the patient is willing to accept. Such a contract allows the patient to remain responsible for his or her behaviors, and encourages appropriate family assistance. Doherty and Baird (1983, 1984) have incorporated this kind of contracting into their detailed protocol for family compliance counseling, which has been adapted to smoking cessation by the family physician Lorne Becker and colleagues (1985) and can be generalized to other risk factors and health promotion activities.

To work effectively with families, the clinician must remain allied with both the patient and the family, and support the patient's autonomy while avoiding taking sides in any conflicts. If the clinician has a long-standing relationship with the individual patient and does not know the family, the family may imagine that the clinician is bringing them in to blame them for the problem. Special efforts must be made to join with the other family members and to acknowledge how much their assistance is needed. On the other hand, if the family has taken a position of overresponsibility for the patient's behavior, they may try to get the physician to join their side of the struggle. The clinician can sometimes engage this overinvolved family by commending them on how much they care about the patient.

For some major life-style changes, families may need additional support from community resources and specialized groups (Alcoholics Anonymous, Weight Watchers, Smoke Enders). Unfortunately, most of these groups do not routinely incorporate families into their programs (although Al-Anon offers a separate group for family members of alcoholics). Many of the techniques of working with individual family members can be incorporated into multifamily groups. We believe that family members should be actively encouraged to participate in the groups. For example, weight reduction programs that give money back to participants who lose weight might want to reward family members who assisted the obese individual.

Dealing with many families seeking major life-style changes can be very demanding and even overwhelming for the clinician. Some disturbed families may be so dysfunctional and rigid that simple, straightforward family interventions are unsuccessful. Individual health professionals should establish a working relationship with a family therapist who can be consulted regularly, and refer the more difficult cases. Some clinicians may want to see some families with a family therapist. Specialized groups and community agencies that deal with health risks should have a family therapist on staff who can assist in running the groups and be available for consultation. Family therapists have expertise in systems theory, family dynamics, and promoting behavior changes—skills that can be invaluable in these settings. Increasingly, family therapists are being trained to deal with health-related problems, and are collaborating with other health professionals. Along with the family therapist/family physician team of Jeri Hepworth and Max Jackson (1985), we believe that the most effective approach to health promotion and risk reduction requires this kind of collaboration.

CONCLUSION

Health promotion and risk reduction within the family are particularly fruitful areas for future research. Most studies have used a simplistic model, viewing families as one source of social support. Researchers must also examine what kinds of interactions within families assist in making life-style changes, and what kinds inhibit life-style changes. How do some families organize themselves around eating, smoking, and exercise patterns? How do some families orient themselves to the outside world and the health care system in a way that allows them flexibility to learn new life-style activities, whereas other families relate to world in ways that foreclose the likelihood of major family life-style changes (Reiss, 1981)? Given that risk factors tend to run in families, family-based intervention programs are likely to be the most cost effective. There is a need to develop and rigorously test such intervention programs. Two areas receiving increasing attention by researchers in the late 1980s are smoking cessation and cholesterol reduction.

Despite the undeniable human and economic value of promoting health and preventing disease, as opposed to treating already existing disease, traditionally less than 2% of the federal health care budget has been devoted to these activities (Dever, 1980). Our society understandably is more enamored of "magic bullets" that attack viruses than of making personally demanding changes in how we live. Until recently, even when clinicians and researchers have addressed life-style issues, they have tended to isolate the individual from the family matrix. This blind spot is beginning to fade. It is becoming clear that without an explicit concern for family dynamics, the road to health promotion and disease prevention is long and rocky. Although a family approach offers no easy success in life-style interventions—no royal road paved in gold—it may offer the best chance of helping motivated people enhance their health and lengthen their life spans.

DISCUSSION QUESTIONS

(1) What are the major life-style changes recommended by the surgeon general? How can the family influence each of these life-style changes?
(2) What are the explanations for the high concordance of cardiovascular

risk factors within families? What are the implications of these findings for health care professionals and for families?

(3) How do health professionals help or hinder families' efforts to change their health risks?

RECOMMENDED READINGS

Califano, J.A.J. (1979). *Healthy People: The Surgeon General's Report on Health Promotion and Disease Prevention*. PHS. DHEW Publication No. 79-55071. Washington, DC: Government Printing Office.

Doherty, W. J., & Baird, M. A. (1983). *Family therapy and family medicine: Toward the primary care of families*. New York: Guilford.

Haynes R. B., Taylor D. W., & Sackett, D. L. (Eds.). (1979). *Compliance in health care*. Baltimore: Johns Hopkins University Press.

CHAPTER

3

Family Vulnerability and Disease Onset

WHY DO SOME SMOKERS DIE from lung cancer or heart disease while others puff away for 60 years and suffer no apparent adverse effects from tobacco use? The answer is that, despite major advances in medical knowledge, we cannot answer the simple question of why one person becomes ill and another does not when they both are exposed to the same disease agents or risk factors. Indeed, all the known biomedical risk factors put together explain only a small amount of the variation in human disease.

Over the past 25 years, there has been increasing interest in the psychosocial environment as it affects susceptibility to illness. There is now substantial evidence to demonstrate that psychosocial stresses have an adverse effect on health (Antonovsky, 1979). Recent studies have shown that social supports have a protective effect, either by buffering the effects of stress or by directly influencing health (Cohen & Syme, 1985). Scientists and clinicians are coming to understand that social factors play an important role in determining who will come down with an illness and who will stay healthy.

As the most intimate social environment, the family is the major source of both stress and social support for most people. This chapter will review the ways in which the family can influence vulnerability to illness and the onset of illness. The topic for special focus will be on what is arguably the most stressful family event—the death of a spouse. We will explore the interactions between families and health care professionals during bereavement, and conclude with implications for family-oriented health care.

FAMILY STRESS

Stress has become a popular lay concept that is now widely accepted by patients as influencing health. Patients present to their physicians with the explanation that because they are "under a lot of stress," their illness (ulcer, back pain, headache) is "acting up." Even traditional scientific medicine is beginning to regard stress as an important aspect of health and illness, particularly in coronary heart disease.

Unfortunately, stress is a concept that is difficult to define and hard to study (Rabkin & Struening, 1976). The most successful method for studying stress has been to examine the impact of important ("stressful") life events and their role in the development of disease. The stress researchers Thomas Holmes and Richard Rahe (1967) pioneered this approach by asking people to rate the amount of social readjustment required for each of 43 common life events (Table 3.1). Each event was given a weighted score based upon how stressful it was perceived to be. The Holmes and Rahe Social Readjustment Scale and similar scales have been used in numerous retrospective and prospective studies to show an increase in stressful life events prior to the development of a wide range of diseases.

Most of the events on the Holmes and Rahe scale occur within the family, and 10 of the 15 most stressful events are family events. This finding suggests that the largest source of stress comes from within the family. Children are likely to be affected by this stress, and a number of studies have looked at the relationship of family life events and child health. In an early study of family stress, the pediatricians Roger Meyer and Robert Haggerty (1962) found that chronic stress was associated with higher rates of streptococcal pharyngitis, and 30% of the strep infections were preceded by a stressful family event. In a large prospective study of preschoolers, family life events were strongly correlated with visits to the physician and hospital admissions for a wide range of conditions (Beautrais et al., 1982). In this study, children from families with more than 12 life events during the four years were six times more likely to be hospitalized.

TABLE 3.1
Life Change Units Measured by the
Social Readjustment Rating Scale

Life Change Events	Values
Family	
death of spouse	100
divorce	73
marital separation	65
death of close family member	63
marriage	50
marital reconciliation	45
major change in health of family	44
pregnancy	40
addition of new family member	39
major change in arguments with wife	35
son or daughter leaving home	29
in-law troubles	29
wife starting or ending work	26
major change in family get-togethers	15
Personal	
detention in jail	63
major personal injury or illness	53
sexual difficulties	39
death of a close friend	37
outstanding personal achievement	28
start or end of formal schooling	26
major change in living conditions	25
major revision of personal habits	24
changing to a new school	20
change in residence	20
major change in recreation	19
major change in church activities	19
major change in sleeping habits	16
major change in eating habits	15
vacation	13
Christmas	12
minor violations of the law	11

(continued)

TABLE 3.1 Continued

Life Change Events	Values
Work	
being fired from work	47
retirement from work	45
major business adjustment	39
changing to a different line of work	36
major change in work responsibilities	29
trouble with boss	23
major change in working conditions	20
Financial	
major change in financial state	38
mortgage or loan over $10,000	31
mortgage foreclosure	30
mortgage or loan less than $10,000	17

SOURCE: Rahe, R. H. (1975). Life changes and near-future illness reports. In L. Levi (Ed.), *Emotions: Their Parameters and Measurement.* New York: Raven Press. Reprinted by permission.

In addition to these studies of total family life events, a number of investigations have examined the effects of specific family life events on health. Research on bereavement, to be reviewed in this chapter, offers the best evidence that family stress affects health. Divorce is also an extremely stressful event in American culture, as indicated by its rank of second on the Holmes and Rahe scale. Several cross-sectional studies (Carter & Glick, 1970; Lynch, 1977; Verbrugge, 1977) have demonstrated an increased mortality rate for all diseases among divorced individuals when compared to the rates for married, single, and widowed people. This complex relationship between marital disruption and health needs to be examined prospectively, however, because of evidence that poor physical health has an adverse effect on marital relationships (Bruhn, 1977; Klein et al., 1968).

Research summarized so far demonstrates that the family events can be a major source of stress, and that this stress can make an individual more susceptible to illness. The next section deals with family as a support factor in preventing disease.

FAMILY AS SOCIAL SUPPORT

John Cassel, an epidemiologist at the University of North Carolina, was instrumental in adapting the epidemiologic model of disease to the study of psychosocial factors in health and disease. He viewed stress as lowering the individual's resistance to illness, and social support as buffering the effects of stress (Cassel, 1976). An extensive body of subsequent research has provided strong evidence to support Cassel's basic contentions that social support can directly improve health, as well as diminish the effects of stress. In most of these studies, the family is the most important source of social support.

Social support is defined by the epidemiologist Lisa Berkman (1984) as "the emotional, instrumental and financial aid that is obtained from one's social network." She further defines social networks as "the web of social ties that surround an individual." Social support thus involves both presence of a social group and a subjective appraisal by the individual about how helpful this group is. Most of the research to date has focused on the presence of potentially supportive relationships (e.g., intact marriage) rather than on the individual's appraisal of these relationships (how supportive the spouse is perceived to be).

In a prospective study of over 6000 adults in Alameda County, California, Berkman and Syme (1979) showed that social network was a major predictor of mortality over a nine-year period. Each measure of social networks was significantly associated with lower mortality, independent of socioeconomic status, previous health status, or health practices. In particular, marital status and contacts with relatives and friends were the most powerful predictors of health. The most socially isolated group had a two to three times greater risk of dying when compared to the least isolated group. In a similar study, the sociologist James House and his colleagues (1982) found a strong association between social isolation and mortality, but for men only. Again, the family components of social support were the most predictive of who would live and who would die.

Studies of social support and mortality in the elderly have shown that the relative importance of different aspects of family support may change over the life span. As part of the Durham County Aging Study in North Carolina, the gerontologist Dan Blazer (1982) found that greater availability, frequency, and positive perception of social support in the elderly were associated with decreased mortality. Those elderly with impaired social support were three times more likely to die during the 30 months of the study than those with good social support. The epidemiologists Dianne Zuckerman, Stanislav Kasl, and Adrian Ostfeld (1984) found a similar relationship among poor elderly residents of New Haven. In both of these studies of the elderly, the presence and number of living children was the most powerful predictor of survival, and marital status per se was not associated with mortality. This finding suggests that children become the most important source of social support for many elderly.

Family support appears to play a particularly important role in the outcome of pregnancy. Women with high levels of stress and low family and social supports have shown higher rates of obstetrical complications (Norbeck & Tilden, 1983; Nuckolls et al., 1972). The family physician Christian Ramsey and colleagues (1986) reported that pregnant women who lived apart from their spouses or families delivered lower birth weight babies than those who lived with a spouse or family. Women who were excessively close or enmeshed with their families, however, also delivered smaller babies, suggesting that the quality as well as the presence of family support influences health. Ramsey and colleagues hypothesized that the family's overinvolvement during pregnancy may be detrimental by not allowing enough autonomy for the expectant mother; metaphorically, one could say that the family did not allow enough "space" for a fully developed new member.

The social support research provides strong and persuasive evidence that social ties and support have a major influence on health (Broadhead et al., 1983), and that the family is the most important element of that support. Many of these studies have used powerful research designs: prospective studies with large numbers of subjects, objective measures of outcome, and control of confounding variables in multivariate analyses. The major weakness of these studies, however, is the use of crude measures of family variables that tell us little about what aspects or qualities of family relationships are most important for preventing disease and premature death.

We turn now to the discussion of bereavement, the most extensively studied topic in this phase of the Family Health and Illness Cycle.

HEALTH CONSEQUENCES OF BEREAVEMENT

Even with our longer life expectancy, bereavement is a highly common occurrence for modern families. An estimated 8 million people—5% to 10% of the U.S. population—lose a close relative each year. The death of a close family member sends reverberations through the family for many years, causing not only emotional suffering but also, according to research studies, adverse health effects on individuals in the family. It is this latter phenomenon—the effect of the loss of a close family member on individuals' vulnerability to illness—that this section will discuss.

The health consequences of bereavement has been extensively investigated (see reviews by Susser, 1981; Jacobs & Ostfeld, 1977; and a report of the National Academy of Sciences—Osterweis et al., 1984). Cross-sectional studies have found that people who have lost a spouse to death have markedly increased death rates for all causes when compared to the married population. In a famous cross-sectional study by the epidemiologists Arthur Kraus and Abraham Lilienfeld (1959), young widowers had 10 times the normal death rate for many physical illnesses.

Prospective studies have also found negative health effects of bereavement, although the adverse effects are of lesser magnitude than those found in the cross-sectional studies. In the psychiatrist C. Murray Parkes's (1969) classic work, London widowers had a 40% higher mortality rate, largely due to heart disease, during the first six months of bereavement when compared to the general population. The best designed and most convincing research on bereavement comes from a population study of Washington County, Maryland. The epidemiologists Knud Helsing and Moyses Szklo (1981) found that, when potential confounding variables (especially smoking and socioeconomic status) were controlled for, widowers showed increased mortality rates, which persisted throughout the 10 years of the study. Widowers who remarried, however, had a subsequent mortality rate lower than the control, nonwidowed group, suggesting that marriage has a protective effect on health, at least for men. Widows in this study suffered no increase in mortality after the death of their spouses.

While numerous studies have described the emotional turmoil associated with bereavement, few have looked systematically at psychiatric morbidity and mortality during this period. Census and survey data have established that suicide rates are higher among the widowed than the married, especially among elderly men. In a study of 320 widows and widowers who committed suicide, MacMahon and Pugh (1965) found that the suicide rate for widowers was 3.5 times that of age-matched controls; widows had twice the normal rate. Alcoholics appear to be at particularly high risk for suicide during bereavement (Murphy & Robins, 1967), and maternal death is a strong risk factor for suicide in young men (Bunch et al., 1971).

Other studies show that widows and widowers increase their use of alcohol, sedatives, and tobacco during the first year of bereavement, but this occurs primarily in those who were already using these substances (Parkes & Brown, 1972). Parkes (1964) found that widows under age 65 were seven times more likely to be prescribed sedatives during the first six months of bereavement than in the period preceding death. Surprisingly, however, there was not an increase in physical symptoms or physician visits during bereavement.

What are the risk factors for adverse consequences of bereavement? Several have been identified. People in poor physical or mental health are more likely to experience worsening of their conditions. Alcoholics are at particular risk for death. Men are more likely to die than women during bereavement, but they are also more likely to remarry. Young widows and widowers appear to suffer more intense bereavement and have more adverse health effects. Spouses who have highly ambivalent relationships appear to do worse during bereavement (Parkes & Weiss, 1983). Studies have not supported the commonly held belief that sudden, unexpected losses are more detrimental than those that are anticipated (Osterweis et al., 1984). Social support does appear to have a positive effect on the health of the bereaved, perhaps by buffering the stress of the grieving process.

BIOLOGICAL CONNECTIONS BETWEEN BEREAVEMENT AND HEALTH

While many studies have explored the health consequences of bereavement, only a few have examined the biological mechanisms by which these effects may occur (Hofer, 1984). An understanding of this process will help in the development of clinical interventions to prevent adverse outcomes. The stress of bereavement may directly affect physiological processes that result in disease or death, or it may affect health behaviors, such as smoking, alcohol consumption, and visits to health professionals, factors that indirectly may lead to illness. There is some evidence for both of these pathways.

Like other stressors, bereavement influences numerous systems of the body. Early stress researchers such as Walter Cannon and Hans

Selye demonstrated that stressful stimuli lead to changes in the autonomic nervous system and the endocrine system. In the "fight-flight" response, large amounts of catecholamines, such as epinephrine (adrenaline) are released into the bloodstream and result in a hyperalert state. Blood pressure and heart rate increase, pupils dilate, blood is shunted away from internal organs to skeletal muscles, and the individual feels fearful or anxious. While this is generally an adaptive response, it can be harmful. In persons with heart disease, the increased stress can lead to a heart attack, arrhythmias, or death (Lown et al., 1980). Engel (1971) studied 170 cases of sudden death and found that 39% of the women and 11% of the men died immediately following the death of someone close. He hypothesized that the deaths were due to cardiac arrests in individuals with preexisting heart disease. In diabetics undergoing significant stress, elevated epinephrine levels cause increased glucose and free fatty acid production and can worsen diabetic control. On this point, the family psychiatrist Salvador Minuchin and colleagues (1978) reported that, in certain psychosomatic families, conflict between family members can elevate fatty acids and precipitate ketoacidosis in diabetics.

Recent interest in biologic mechanisms has focused on changes in the immune system and its effect on the development of cancer and infections. Studies in animals and humans have demonstrated that immune function is directly influenced by the nervous system, and that stress can lead to immunosuppression and an increase in illness (Ader, 1981). The T-lymphocytes, the mediators of cellular immunity, are the most susceptible to stress and play a major role in defense against cancer and certain infections. The B lymphocytes, which produce antibodies, appear to be less influenced by stress.

Two well-controlled studies have shown that there is a decrease in immunity during bereavement. The Australian immunologist R. W. Bartrop and colleagues (1977) found that the T-lymphocytes of 26 recently bereaved spouses had lower responsiveness than the lymphocytes of a matched control group. The psychiatrist Steven Schleifer and colleagues (1983) monitored the immune functioning of 20 spouses of women with advanced breast cancer. In men whose spouses died during the study period, there was a significant drop in T-lymphocyte responsiveness during the two months of bereavement. *Psychoimmunology*, the term for the field that studies these phenomena, is making exciting strides that promise to advance our understanding of the relationship between the mind and body and social system.

In addition to biological changes, bereavement is associated with profound behavioral changes, which can also have an effect on health. As discussed earlier, the bereaved increase their use of tobacco, alcohol, and sedatives. Smoking is a major risk factor for heart disease and the numerous cancers that are increased during bereavement. Alcohol abuse has many physical, psychological, and social sequelae. Cirrhosis, accidents, and suicides, a triple threat that accounts for large part of the increased mortality after bereavement, are commonly associated with alcohol abuse or alcoholism. These changes in health behaviors may be more important clinically than the direct physiologic effects of bereavement.

Bereavement is a natural human experience, an inevitable one for people who live long enough to survive their loved ones. Some individuals experience the emotional pain and the attendant biological disturbances without lasting ill effects. Others experience serious illness and premature death. Evidence at hand suggests that a socially supportive network may be a key factor in how well a person handles bereavement. Because health professionals are involved so closely with the dying process, they are a potentially important part of the individual's bereavement support system. We turn now to the discussion of health professionals' dealings with bereaved people.

HEALTH PROFESSIONALS AND THE
FAMILY DURING BEREAVEMENT

Death and dying are not only stressful times for families, but also for health professionals. It is a time when communication between the clinician and the family is the most crucial. This section describes some aspects of the physician-family interactions before and after the death of a family member. Unfortunately, there are no systematic studies of the role of the health care provider at the time of a patient's death and during bereavement, but anecdotal reports and clinical experiences of the authors suggest that breakdowns in communications, misunderstandings, and unmet needs are common between clinicians and families.

Many clinicians have great difficulty dealing with death, whether it occurs in their practices or in their own families (Tolle et al., 1984). For some, fear of death was a reason to chose the health care field, either as a way of denying death by trying to conquer it, or as a way to work through unresolved issues concerning death. These clinicians may have experienced the loss of a close family member when they were young. For example, an oncology nurse we know decided on her career as a young girl, shortly after her older brother died of leukemia. She specializes in working with the families of dying children.

For most health professionals and especially physicians, a primary goal is to preserve life, and death is often viewed as failure. It is usually associated with guilt, even when appropriate care is given. Physicians' feelings of overresponsibility, high expectations, and omnipotence lead to the sense that they "should" be able to prevent death. When a delay in diagnosis or an error in treatment occurs, no matter how insignificant, this guilt is amplified many times (Hilfiker, 1984). As part of this guilt, physicians often believe that family members blame them for the death. These feelings can interfere with the clinician's ability to work with the family. For example, a pediatric oncologist explained that one of the reasons that the primary care pediatricians referred the total care of their cancer patients to the specialists was a sense of guilt for not picking up the cancer sooner.

Dealing with death in clinical practice can be physically and emotionally exhausting. Clinicians may choose a specialty partly based upon whether they will care for dying patients. In obstetrics and general pediatrics, death is rare but tragic, while it is common in geriatrics and oncology. Frequent exposure to death does not necessarily make health professionals more comfortable or skilled in working with dying patients and their families. Some clinicians develop very strong defenses and avoid any issues around death, focusing only on the medical treatments. In extreme cases, the clinician may not tell the patient the diagnosis, may continue aggressive treatment beyond when it is indicated, may refuse to acknowledge that the patient is dying, and may avoid the patient and family when death is near.

These extreme responses to the dying patient are becoming increasingly rare in health care. More attention is being paid to the psychosocial needs of the dying patient (Cassem & Stewart, 1975; Friel, 1983), although the needs of the family are still being neglected. Family members sometimes are seen as intruders in the hospital, disrupting the usual routines. They may be only allowed to visit at certain times, and only two or three at a time. Children are not allowed on many hospital wards. Most rooms do not have enough chairs for the family to sit around the patient's bed. The health care providers commonly ignore family members visiting in the hospital, rarely introducing themselves or asking who the family member is. Most hospital charts contain very little family information, other than who is the next of kin. A family history of inheritable illnesses may be recorded, but the inclusion of psychosocial information is uncommon. More than 80% of Americans die in hospitals, and these institutions remain preoccupied with the biological needs of individual dying patients. Families frequently are left to fend for themselves.

A notable exception to the exclusion and neglect of families in hospitals is on the pediatrics and obstetrical wards. Pediatrics has lead the way in involving parents in the day-to-day care of their hospitalized child. Parents are encouraged to stay with their child as much as possible and are often provided with cots to sleep in the child's room. They may help with feedings and simple medical procedures, particularly ones that will have to be continued after discharge. In obstetrics, fathers are routinely present at the time of birth. Many hospitals have built "family birthing centers," where the entire family, including children and grandparents, can participate in the labor and delivery. What has been accomplished in the family-centered care of hospitalized children and pregnant women needs to be extended to all patients.

During the terminal phases of an illness, a common response of the health professionals is gradually to withdraw from the patient and family. Less time is spent with the patient in the hospital, or visits are scheduled less often, as illustrated in the following case.

CASE ILLUSTRATION 1

A 60-year-old woman was admitted to the hospital with long-standing and increasing back pain. A diagnostic evaluation revealed lung cancer with metastases to the spine. Despite radiation therapy, nerve blocks, and high dose narcotics, she remained in severe pain during the last month of her life in the hospital. After her initial evaluation and unsuccessful attempts to relieve the pain, her physician became increasingly uncomfortable and depressed seeing her. Visits became shorter and less frequent. He became less attentive to her palliative care. She died while he was out of town, and because of communication difficulties with the physician covering, the family was not notified for two days.

This withdrawal or disengagement is a premature separation from the patient that stems from a combination of fear of death and guilt over a failure to prevent death. The clinician may not even be aware of this withdrawal taking place and may rationalize that there is not much he or she can do for the patient. If the clinician is conscious of the discomfort of caring for a dying patient, it may increase the sense of guilt ("Not only am I unable to prevent death, but I cannot adequately care for the patient during death").

In other situations, the health professional may become *overinvolved* with the dying patient and the family. The clinician feels compelled to save the patient and responsible for the total care of the patient, and may even recommend unproven or inappropriate treatment.

CASE ILLUSTRATION 2

A five-year-old girl, Becky, was diagnosed with a brain tumor after presenting with headaches and strabismus (crossed eyes). Over 18 months, she had a progressively downhill course, despite radiation and chemotherapy, and died. Her primary care nurse, who also had a five-year-old daughter named Becky, was involved in all aspects of the girl's treatment, making frequent home visits, encouraging consultations and second opinions, and double checking the care of the consulting physicians. When there were mixups in communication between consultants or in the patient's care, the nurse became furious with the physicians and the other nursing care providers. When the child finally died, the nurse was unable to work for more than a week, and began considering switching to a less stressful unit in the hospital.

In cases such as this, the clinician becomes part of the family and reacts much as family members do. The inability to prevent death is particularly painful, and the clinician may blame him- or herself or other providers. In the latter case, it may lead to splitting of the health care team with one or more providers identifying themselves as protecting the interests of the patient and the family against the rest of the health care system. Or the clinician may view the family as not caring enough or providing what the patient needs, and may join in a coalition with the patient against the rest of the family. As the family psychiatrist Murray Bowen (1976) points out, the strong emotional responses of clinicians and family around the time of death can distort communication and lead to conflicts and the formation of coalitions within both groups.

Unfortunately, many dying patients are not cared for by their primary care physician or nurse, or indeed anyone who knows them and their family. In most major medical centers, patients are cared for by a team of health professionals, including nurses, resident physicians, and consultants, with no single provider identified as being in charge. The family's contact is primarily through the resident physicians who change periodically. Poor communication and confusion occur commonly in these cases. The patient and family may not receive a full explanation of the illness, its prognosis, and treatment options. On occasion, the diagnosis of a terminal illness is given to the family but not the patient, or vice versa. Questions regarding how aggressive treatment should be and whether the patient wishes to be resuscitated in the event of a cardiac arrest are often avoided.

The lack of attention to the needs of families is most apparent at the time of death. Many health professionals believe that their responsibilities are limited to patients, and their involvement ceases with the death of the patient. The family may be notified of the death by someone whom they do not know. This stranger then asks for permission for an autopsy or organ donation. If the family is not at the hospital at the time of death, the body may have already been removed to the morgue by the time the family arrives to make their goodbyes to the deceased.

Health care professionals and particularly physicians are not trained to assist grieving families. They may feel uncomfortable being with crying family members who are in pain. As mentioned before, they may feel guilty about their inability to prevent the death. Or they may feel completely helpless, unable previously to prevent the death and unable now to remove the pain of the survivors. Physicians tend to be action oriented, and there is a tremendous urge to "do something." This leads to premature reassurance ("he never suffered"), advice giving ("try not to think about it"), or prescriptions for sedatives. These are rarely helpful and indeed can do harm by interfering with the normal grieving process. Some clinicians, fortunately, are able to give families what they need most during the bereavement period: empathic listening without comments or suggestions.

Family problems and dysfunctions usually become worse or more apparent during the terminal phase of an illness or during bereavement. Conflicts among family members may be more overt and become focused upon the patient. Arguments about who has cared most for the patient, who will provide the terminal care, what will happen to the patient's possessions, and concerns about inheritance may arise. Family members may try to get the clinician to take sides in these conflicts. They may call the clinician and complain about other family members. Most clinicians have not been trained in how to assess family problems and how to decide which they can manage and which require referral to a family therapist.

After the acute phase, continued care and support for the grieving family is not a common occurrence in American health care. In a study of physician-family communication following a death, one-half of the surviving spouses reported no contact in the subsequent year with the physician who cared for the deceased. This occurred despite the fact that 55% of the spouses still had unanswered questions about the death one year later. None of the physicians attended the funeral (Tolle et al., 1986). In another survey, only 6% of physicians indicated that they routinely contacted families after the funeral, and less than 10% reported sending a card or attending the funeral (Tolle et al., 1984). Clearly, there is a need for more contact between clinicians and families after a death, and the benefits may accrue to both parties.

IMPLICATIONS FOR THE
HEALTH PROFESSIONAL

There is very little research literature to guide a discussion of how clinicians should interact with families around issues of death and dying. The following discussion is based primarily on our clinical experience and our own values about dealing with families.

For clinicians to deal adequately with dying patients and their families, they must be relatively comfortable with death and have faced their own issues around death. If the clinician has unresolved issues concerning deaths in his or her family of origin, these must be dealt with. Caring for dying patients or grieving families can be extremely stressful, and clinicians must have access to support and assistance from colleagues. They need the opportunity to discuss difficult cases, share feelings of guilt or inadequacy, and at times receive advice. While it is common for clinicians to discuss cases with colleagues, it is usually restricted to biomedical aspects of the case, and rarely involves sharing of emotional reactions. One pediatric residency program has developed a seminar for helping interns care for dying children and their families (Berman & Villarreal, 1983). Participants reported that they gained a better understanding of their own feelings toward death, which enabled them to cope better with the stress of caring for dying children. The family therapist Susan McDaniel and colleagues (1986) have described the use of a group of health professionals to provide a biopsychosocial consultation for difficult medical cases. In addition to providing an opportunity for ventilation, mutual support, and assistance with diagnosis and treatment planning, the group explores how the health provider's own family dynamics are influencing each case.

After a death, the clinician also is bereaved (Pasnau & Hollingsworth, 1977). To be of assistance to the grieving family, the health professional must attend to his or her own grief. Health professionals tend to minimize the impact of deaths of their patients by discussing only the medical aspects of the death. We believe that clinicians should take time to say goodbye to their dying patients, and when possible to attend their funerals. If the clinician is feeling uncertain or guilty about the death, then discussion of the case with colleagues is crucial. Mistakes are particularly torturous for clinicians to handle, particularly in our current malpractice climate, which offers little opportunity for confession or forgiveness (Hilfiker, 1984).

During the terminal phases of an illness, it is crucial for one clinician, usually the primary care physician, to assume responsibility for coordinating care and communicating directly with the patient and family. Ideally, this clinician, along with the patient's primary nurse, should meet regularly with the patient and family together to discuss prognosis and treatment of the illness. At the time of death, the family should be notified as soon as possible, and given the opportunity to view the body and say their goodbyes (Hollingsworth & Pasnau, 1977). The request for an autopsy or for organ donation should be made by the primary care physician. In addition to providing information about cause of death, the health professional needs to be available and supportive to the family, allowing them to share their grief unencumbered by the physician's desire to reassure or explain or prescribe. When physicians and nurses rise to this challenge, they experience the sweet sorrow that comes from aiding a family in its early grief.

The use of psychotropic medication during the bereavement period is controversial. Sedatives and hypnotics, primarily benzodiazepines such as Valium, are the most common drugs used. As indicated before, studies have demonstrated increased use during bereavement (Parkes, 1964), and those who start using them at this time are likely to remain on them for at least two years (O'Brien, 1986). Sedatives can help bereaved family members feel better over the short term, with less overt distress and crying. Many experts, however, believe that sedatives may inhibit the normal grieving process and lead to unresolved grief reactions (Osterweis et al., 1984). It is particularly important not to give these medications for use during the funeral or wake, as the sedated individual may not remember these important events. Antidepressants and antipsychotics are rarely indicated during bereavement, except in cases where serious psychiatric illness emerges.

Most bereaved families receive considerable support during the first few weeks after the death. After a month or two, friends stop calling and may expect the bereaved to stop grieving and "get on with living." They may even try to cheer up the bereaved person and get him or her to start socializing more. These attempts at helping usually backfire for they occur too soon, and they make the bereaved feel unsupported. It is during this time that the continued involvement of the health professionals is crucial. If the clinician has cared for the patient and the family for a considerable period of time before the loss and then does not make any further contacts, the family may perceive this as an additional loss.

We recommend that the health professional follow up with the bereaved family by phone calls, office visits, or home visits. Phone calls every two to three weeks for the first few months can be used to inquire about other family members and answer questions. Ideally, an office visit should be scheduled for four to six weeks after the death. This visit can be used to review the autopsy results, if one was obtained, or other aspects of the death. Some discussion of normal bereavement is useful. Bereaved family members may feel that they are "going crazy" because of crying spells, lack of energy, or preoccupation with the deceased. Normalizing these symptoms can be very therapeutic. At this time, some assessment of how well the bereaved family is coping can be made. Signs of abnormal grief include persistent compulsive overactivity without a sense of loss; identification with the deceased and acquisition of symptoms belonging to the last illness of the deceased; deterioration of health in the survivors; social isolation, withdrawal, or alienation; and severe depression (Lindemann, 1944). Family members with evidence of pathological grief reactions should be referred for more extensive evaluation and treatment.

At two to four months after the death, family members should be encouraged to have a complete physical examination. Bereavement is stressful and numerous studies reviewed earlier have demonstrated that the bereaved are at higher risk for illness and death. As part of the assessment of how the family is coping, questions about the increased use of alcohol, drugs, or tobacco should be asked. Alcohol and drug abuse may begin during this period.

Most bereaved families adapt well without any formal interventions from health professionals. Some family members, however, may benefit from referral for counseling. Bereavement counseling is done by nearly all schools of psychotherapy. They differ in their theoretical orientations, length of therapy, and goals. Counseling may be done by the primary care clinician, a mental health worker, a member of the clergy, or a lay counselor. When referring for psychotherapy, it is helpful to get the whole family involved in the initial evaluation. The family member with the identified problem may be expressing the grief for the rest of the family, who may be unable to grieve. Other family members may be trying to cheer up the identified patient and thus be part of the problem.

These recommendations for the care of the grieving family are based upon our clinical experience and on the existing clinical literature. Unfortunately, there has been no research on the impact of these family interventions. The little research that has been done on care of the bereaved has examined the impact of individual counseling and support groups rather than family interventions.

Over the past decade, there has been a tremendous growth in mutual support or self-help groups. They exist for nearly every disorder or condition. The most successful group for the bereaved has been the Widow to Widow Program (Silverman, 1970). Started in Boston in the late 1960s, the program has spread across the country under the sponsorship of the American Association of Retired Persons. In addition to emotional support, specific information is provided to help the widow cope. Several aspects of these programs are unique. They are outreach programs, so that widows do not have to seek out any assistance. Support is provided by lay persons, so that there is no stigma of psychiatric care. All contact in the program is one on one. Widows do not seem to be interested in joining groups. The first contact with the widow is not made until six weeks after the death, when studies have shown that intervention is most likely to be accepted. The primary goal of these programs is not recovery, but adaptation to a new condition—widowhood.

CONCLUSION

Scientists and clinicians are beginning to discover the complex web that interconnects the body, the mind, and the social group. We believe that family life is the crucible where these three dimensions of human life are joined most forcefully. Our families make us vulnerable to disease at times of family stress, and they protect us from disease at times of personal misfortune. Loss of a family member is the perhaps greatest threat to individual and family well-being, and it is here that the family most compellingly needs nurturing from its wider network of kin, friends, professionals, and community. As health care professionals grope slowly toward a deeper understanding of the interconnections of human life, there is hope that they can participate more fully in the healing family process of dying and learning to live anew.

DISCUSSION QUESTIONS

(1) In what ways can the family be a source of stress for individuals and thereby affect their health? How does the social support of the family influence health?

(2) What are the major physical and emotional health consequences of bereavement? What factors might lessen the adverse health effects of bereavement?

(3) What are some common problems experienced by health professionals caring for dying patients and their families? How can these difficulties be addressed constructively by these professionals and by health care institutions?

RECOMMENDED READINGS

Antonovsky, A. (1979). *Health, stress, and coping.* San Francisco: Jossey-Bass.

Cohen S., & Syme, S. L. (Eds.). (1985). *Social support and health.* Orlando, FL: Academic Press.

Hollingsworth, C. E., & Pasnau, R. O. (Eds.). (1977). *The family in mourning: A guide for health professionals.* New York: Grune & Stratton.

Osterweis M., Soloman, F., & Green, M. (Eds.). (1984). *Bereavement: Reactions, consequences, and care.* Washington, DC: National Academy Press.

CHAPTER

4

Family Illness Appraisal

HEALTH APPRAISAL OR DIAGNOSIS is regarded commonly as a process handled by physicians and other health professionals. In this stereotyped view, individuals experience symptoms that cause them discomfort and then go to a physician for diagnosis and treatment of the problem. Assessment is a professional activity requiring extensive professional training; the patient's job is to accept the doctor's decisions about the problem and its solution.

The reality is that the appraisal of health symptoms is a complex personal and social activity that goes on largely outside professional settings. A large number of studies, many of them involving families keeping daily health diaries, attest to the fact that health problems are quite plentiful and that most never end up in a doctor's office. The family physician Raymond Demers and colleagues (1980) asked 107 individuals to keep health diaries over a three-week period. The sample consisted of a healthy, well-educated group enrolled in a prepaid health insurance plan. The researchers found that individuals experienced at least one health problem on approximately half of all study days. Another study of low-income families by the pediatrician Joel Albert found an even greater number of illness days (Albert, Kosa, & Haggerty, 1967).

What are the leading symptoms experienced by individuals in these studies? Respiratory problems, gastrointestinal problems, accident or injury, skin problems, emotional/psychological problems, and headaches. Given the prevalence of health problems reported by individuals, it is not surprising that few of these problems are brought to a physician: people would end up spending hours every week in a doctor's office. In the Demers et al. (1980) study, less than 6% of the reported problems received professional medical attention, and this was in a setting where patients were not charged for office visits, telephone calls, and most medications. Other studies reviewed by the medical sociologist I. K. Zola (1972) report that between 10% and 30% of health problems are brought to professional attention.

What are people doing with their symptoms if not calling the doctor? A large number of studies by medical sociologists and anthropologists demonstrate that individuals tend to evaluate their health symptoms through discussions with family and close friends (Albert et al., 1967; Kasl & Cobb, 1966; Litman, 1974). This intimate network helps the individual to determine the nature and severity of the problem, and to decide whether professional attention is required. Most of the time, both the diagnosis and the treatment are handled within the family. Professionals, then, assess health problems referred by families.

A concept used by Doherty and Baird (1983) to describe the central family member who influences health appraisal is the "family health expert." Although the description of this role is based more on clinical observation than on direct research data, Doherty and Baird believe that in most families an individual family member is assigned the role of expert in health matters. Traditionally, the wife/mother in the family often plays this role, as does grandmother, but the role may also be played by male or female family members who are health professionals. From a clinical viewpoint, the family health expert may be the key family member for the clinician to make contact with in arriving at a consensual diagnosis and treatment plan for the patient. In everyday matters of health and illness, the grandmother's authority may be greater than the doctor's.

The social process of illness appraisal, then, seems to occur primarily within families, perhaps influenced most strongly by the family health expert. How do families differ from professionals in approaching illness appraisal? Or, in Kleinman's (1980) term, how do families' "explanatory models" for illness and treatment differ from professionals' explanatory models? The following case illustrations show some common differences in operation.

CASE ILLUSTRATION 1

At 2:00 a.m., Dr. Crosby is called to the emergency room to treat Jennifer Scott, a six-year-old with a fever and sore throat. In the examining room with Jennifer are her distraught parents, who are convinced that their child has a serious disease. They tell Dr. Crosby that they first noticed the child's fever at bedtime, around 9:00 p.m. When Jennifer couldn't sleep because of her discomfort, they decided to bring her to the emergency room. The staff there called Dr. Crosby, their family doctor. Physical examination reveals a temperature of 101 degrees, a slightly red throat, and no other signs of disease. Exasperated and sleepy, Dr. Crosby angrily asks the parents why they brought the child to the emergency room at this hour for a low-grade fever and minor sore throat. The parents defensively reply that the fever was higher a few hours ago, and ask the doctor if he can run some tests to make sure she is OK. The doctor responds that tests would be a waste of money. He tells them to give Jennifer Tylenol and bring her to the office in three days if her sore throat has not improved. The parents, not knowing whether to feel relieved that Jennifer does not have a serious problem or sorry that she didn't have a problem serious enough for Dr. Crosby's approval, quietly leave by the patient exit, while Dr. Crosby bangs the door of the doctor's exit as he hurriedly leaves for home.

CASE ILLUSTRATION 2

The next morning, Mrs. Erskine brings four-year-old Johnny to Dr. Crosby because Johnny is complaining of an earache. Dr. Crosby diagnoses acute otitis media and prescribes a ten-day course of an antibiotic. He asks them to return in two weeks for follow-up.

After failing to keep the follow-up appointment, mother and child return four weeks later complaining that Johnny's earache is back. Upon inquiry, Dr. Crosby finds out that Mrs. Erskine gave Johnny the medicine for only four to five days, until his symptoms cleared up. Dr. Crosby recalls that he has had this kind of trouble with Mrs. Erskine frequently in the past: She skips doctor-recommended office visits, neglects well-child checkups, and decides for herself how much she will comply with doctors' prescriptions. Frustrated about his inability to manage Johnny's chronic ear problems, Dr. Crosby has little patience for what he perceives as Mrs. Erskine's irresponsibility in the health care of her child. He angrily tells her that he will not be responsible for her son's ear problems unless she cooperates by giving the medicine as prescribed. Mrs. Erskine timidly agrees to do better, and leaves the office thinking about where she can bring her son for better medical care for his ear problems.

Although there is considerable variation among families and among professionals in explanatory models for assessing health and illness, we nevertheless believe that the following two differences occur between most families and most health professionals trained in the biomedical model in contemporary North American culture:

(1) Emphasis on the subjective versus the objective. Clinicians are trained to look for measurable biological changes associated with disease, such as bacteria in the blood or urine, and elevated blood pressure or blood glucose. Reports of illness not accompanied by such objective biological indices do not fit well into the biomedical explanatory model of most contemporary physicians (Engel, 1977). Individuals and families, on the other hand, tend to focus more on the subjective aspects of illness. The leading immediate issue is the extent of pain and discomfort in the family member. Families may also respond strongly to overt physical signs such as body temperature that may be of only minor importance to clinicians. In the first vignette above, the parents' explanatory model emphasized the child's subjective discomfort and the presence of an elevated temperature, whereas the physician found no objective indicators of serious biological disease.

Beyond the immediate subjective distress related to the symptoms, the psychiatrist Z. J. Lipowski (1969) has proposed that individuals and families ascribe four meanings to illness: *threat* (to life, or to functioning in some area of life); *loss* (of functioning, of a role); *gain* (relief from an unwanted role); and *insignificance*. Clinicians can be said to ascribe the same four meanings, not always concordant with those of the patient and family. What to a clinician might be an insignificant health problem (say, a minor sore throat and low-grade fever) might threaten the family's sense of the future welfare of a child. And what to a family might be an insignificant issue of elevated blood pressure in a family member who feels fine might to a clinician be a serious threat to the survival of the patient. Clearly, this situation is rife with potential for misunderstanding and conflict.

(2) Interpersonal framework versus epidemiological framework. Clinicians are trained to evaluate symptoms in terms of the probability that they are associated with certain diseases. (*Epidemiology* studies the incidence and prevalence of disease in a population.) A fever, for example, is a very common, nonspecific symptom that accompanies a

wide variety of disease and nondisease states. Physicians nowadays tend not to be concerned about fevers unless they are accompanied by other symptoms or occur in infants. Families, on the other hand, tend to think of fevers in terms of the experiences of other family members and close friends. If Cousin Freddie's simple fever six months ago ended up in meningitis, then for that family the incidence of serious disease underlying fever is quite high. What to an epidemiologist might be a probability of, say, 1 in 1000 that the child's fever signaled the onset of meningitis, to the family might be a probability of 1 in 10, given that Freddie is one of ten children in the close family system. Similarly, if no one in the family's memory has died of a stroke, the clinician's dire warnings about high blood pressure and the probability of stroke may fall prey to the family's own interpersonal epidemiology.

The next section of this chapter reviews in more detail the most intensely studied health appraisal made by families, namely, whether to consult a physician for a child's illness.

PARENTS' AND CHILDREN'S
USE OF MEDICAL CARE

As mentioned before, the idealized professional model of health care utilization suggests that parents evaluate the child's symptoms objectively and, when appropriate, bring the child to the doctor's office for professional evaluation. Both clinical experience and research studies refute this notion. This section reviews several prominent studies in this area.

A fascinating study by Klaus Roghmann and Robert Haggerty (1973), from the University of Rochester's Department of Pediatrics, has helped to tease out the association between a child's illness and the decision by parents to seek medical attention for their child. Mothers in 512 randomly selected families agreed to keep health diaries on themselves and their children for 28 consecutive days. They recorded upsetting events in the family, the presence of illness, and any use of health services by family members. Findings showed that *in the absence of recorded illness*, the presence of stress in the family increased the probability of utilization (30% for mothers, 9% for children). Interestingly, in the *presence* of illness, stress as expected increased the probability of utilization for children (23%) but *decreased* the probability of utilization for mothers (–15%). The authors interpreted this last finding as follows:

> Mothers, especially, may recognize stress as a cause of their own illness and do not regard it as legitimate to take the sick role for such illness. They do, however, regard it as legitimate to assign the sick role to their children for stress-related illness and actually do so more frequently for such illness than for stress-unrelated illness. (Roghmann & Haggerty, 1973, p. 524)

When parents bring their child to a doctor, generally the focus of the interview is on the physical symptoms of the child rather than on the concerns of the parents (Korsch & Negrette, 1972). What are parents' often unspoken concerns that lead them to bring their child to a doctor? The physicians Lee Bass and Richard Cohen (1982) investigated parents' "actual reasons for coming" when they brought their sick children for medical attention. In their study of 370 sick-patient visits in a pediatric practice, the authors asked parents two questions in addition to the routine medical questions: "What are you concerned about?" and "Is there anything special about the problem that causes your concern?" These questions elicited several previously unverbalized issues, including family history of serious or life-threatening illnesses, fear of loss and separation, fear of the child's death, and the fear of another family member who was pressing for "answers" about the child's symptoms. In a similar vein, psychologists Dennis Turk, Mark Litt, and Peter Salovey (1985) reported that in a lower socioeconomic status group, family history of a similar problem was one of the leading predictors of mothers' use of urgent treatment for their children.

Parents' own utilization of health care has been used in several studies as an indirect measure of parental beliefs and attitudes toward health care. The health policy scholars Paul Newacheck and Neal Halfon (1986) examined the association between mothers' and children's utilization of physicians in a large sample from the National Health Interview Survey. Results indicated that the mother's use pattern was a better predictor of the likelihood that her child would see a doctor over a year's time than was the child's own measured health status. This finding is in accord with a study by the community medicine scholar Marian Osterweis and her colleagues (1979), who showed that other family members' medicine use was a strong predictor of each individual's medicine use—a better predictor even than the individual's own level of morbidity or illness. In other words, these studies suggest that, beyond the presence of illness in the child, the parents' own use of health services is an important determinant of the child's use of health services.

Most research on parents' influence on children's use of health care has relied on mothers' reports. In many studies, *parent* means *mother*. There is relatively little research on fathers' influence on their children's health care. Two exceptions showed contradictory results. The epidemiologist Herman Tyroler and his colleagues (1965) found similarities in preventive health behaviors (such as immunizations and use of dental services) among father-mother-child triads. Mother-child pairs were found most similar, father-mother pairs intermediate, and father-child pairs lowest in similarity. The researcher concluded that fathers' influence on children is much less than mothers' influence. The epidemiologist T. Ann Gorton and her colleagues (1979) examined the similarity in two illness behaviors among family members in a community population: number of symptoms and number of doctor visits during a four-week period. The authors hypothesized that the mother-child pairs would be most similar in the two illness behaviors. They found, however, that father-child pairs were most similar and that mother-child pairs did not differ from similarity one would expect by chance. These researchers concluded that fathers' health behaviors may have more influence on children than previous research had indicated.

With such limited and contradictory findings on the unique influence of fathers on children's health care, no clear conclusions are possible. Clearly, there is need for more studies that consider fathers as full-fledged parents in studies of family and health.

In summary, the family's appraisal of the health of a family member, and the family's decision to pursue medical care, often have little to do with the objective physical status that is of primary interest to many clinicians. Most people experience distressing physical symptoms on a frequent basis, but handle these problems at home rather than at the doctor's office. As the family physician Michael Glenn (1984, p. 41) observes: "Families usually have rules determining how intense pain must be before anyone will grant it legitimacy, how intense it must be before anyone will be brought to a physician." When family members do go to the doctor, the nature of the physical symptoms is just one factor in the decision—and presumably reflects just one of several needs to be met in the clinical encounter.

CLINICIAN-FAMILY INTERACTIONS
AROUND HEALTH APPRAISAL

Earlier in this chapter, we referred to clinical diagnosis as the professional analogue to family health appraisal. We mentioned that many clinicians, especially physicians, hold a fairly narrow biomedical explanatory model of illness and treatment. We reviewed studies on the complexities of the family's appraisal processes. Based on this discussion, it should not be surprising that many clinician/patient/family interactions lack the cooperation for which clinicians wish. When patients do not adhere to the clinician's advice about managing an illness, clinicians generally use the term *noncompliance*. The magnitude of patient noncompliance is well documented in modern medicine, particularly by the public health team of Haynes, Taylor, and Sackett. Hypertension provides a good illustration because it is a readily diagnosed, serious medical problem with treatment regimens of proven effectiveness. A variety of studies by public health scholars and health psychologists have shown that over 50% of hypertensive patients are likely to discontinue therapy within one year of starting (Caldwell et al., 1970; Wilber & Barrows, 1972). Among patients who remain in treatment, an estimated 40% fail to take enough medicine to achieve adequate blood pressure control (McKenney et al., 1973). A commonly used rule of thumb among researchers who study hypertension compliance is that only one-fourth of hypertensives are actually under treatment and that only one-half of those are actually controlling their blood pressure (McKenney et al., 1973).

Aside from this empirical evidence that all is not well in terms of cooperation between patients and clinicians, there is not much research available to guide our discussion of interactions between health professionals and families, or of family interventions in the health appraisal area. Hence, these discussions, like a number of others in this volume, are based heavily on the authors' experience, opinions, and values, supported by the available pertinent literature.

CASE ILLUSTRATION 3

Mr. S., a 55-year-old male, comes to see Dr. Crosby for an employment physical. His blood pressure is 160/105, and Dr. Crosby tells him that he may have hypertension and asks him to return for further blood pressure checks to confirm the diagnosis. When Mr. S. arrives home and tells his wife and teenage children that the doctor thinks he may have hypertension, they scoff at the idea. Nobody in the family has ever had that problem, they say, and besides, Mr. S. is the least tense (as in "hypertense") person they know. His wife assures him that his blood pressure must have been raised by the fight he had yesterday at work with his boss. Mr. S. fails to keep his return appointment with Dr. Crosby.

As with the previous two cases in this chapter, Mr. S.'s interaction with the health care system involved the covert clash of health appraisal frameworks or explanatory models (Kleinman, 1980). Every family can be viewed as its own culture, and families tend to cluster into more or less identifiable ethnic and cultural groups. Clearly, the cultural diversity among patients and their families is far greater than that among physicians and other health professionals who tend to be primarily White, middle class, and oriented to a scientific/rationalist framework.

What happens when the family's explanatory model clashes with the dominant biomedical model of the clinician? The first likely outcome is misunderstanding, followed by lack of cooperation, and ending in negative labeling and frustration. The three most common labels, in our experience, are *stupid*, *irresponsible*, and *overprotective*. Stupidity is ascribed when patients and families do not change their behavior in the face of clear presentations of facts by the clinician. The hypertensive Mr. S. and his family described above would be regarded as stupid. In the case of the child with ear problems, previously cited in this chapter, the mother, Mrs. Erskine, would be labeled "irresponsible": She is too lazy or careless to give her child the proper dose of antibiotic. In the case of the Scotts, the distraught parents who brought their daughter to the emergency room, the parents would be labeled "overprotective." A more dramatic case reported in the media in the early 1980s concerned a child whose parents refused chemotherapy for his leukemia. When the court ordered the parents to allow the boy to be given chemotherapy, they took him to Mexico for Laetrile treatments. The media almost universally labeled the parents as "stupid" and "irresponsible."

Patients, of course, have their own labels for clinicians, especially physicians, with whom they have these negative interactions. Some of the printable labels are *insensitive*, *rude*, *arrogant*, and *patronizing*.

What further complicates this negative clinical picture is the tendency of American physicians to assume personal responsibility for the sickness and health of their patients. Thus the patient's and family's noncompliance may be seen by the physician as a personal affront: The physician has been trained to cure disease by rational means, and these people are standing in the way of the doctor's needs for control and success. To their credit, physicians and other health professionals care greatly about their ability to alleviate suffering associated with disease. To perceive their time and training to be misused, as in the cases cited above, is intensely frustrating to many clinicians. In the clash between family culture and professional culture, the family culture nearly always comes out looking bad, at least in the eyes of some health professionals. The clinician may win the argument, but the family follows its own path and ultimately frustrates the clinician.

Many times the clash of explanatory models occurs around issues on which there has been change in professional judgment. In the 1940s and 1950s, pediatricians waged a major public campaign about the risk of rheumatic fever from strep throat, and encouraged parents to have their children examined if they develop a sore throat. Because the risk of rheumatic fever has fallen so drastically, it is no longer clear that the benefits of treating strep throat outweigh the risks. Many physicians now try to discourage patients from coming in for throat cultures when their children have sore throats. An example of a more drastic change in the medical community is that of tonsillectomies, which not long ago were almost universally recommended and now are almost universally discouraged. Once the new medical opinion is firm, clinicians frequently assume that patients and families will fall into line. Families, however, have long memories in health matters; several generations have learned the previous medical conventional wisdom and blended this knowledge with their family wisdom. It is unrealistic to expect them to change rapidly.

A common example of this process has occurred with the regular changes in medical opinion about infant feeding. When infant formula was first developed, physicians promoted it as better than breast milk, and mothers were encouraged to begin solid food in the first few months of life. As the benefits of breast-feeding have become evident, mothers are now being encouraged to breast-feed and to withhold solids as long as possible. Some experts, however, are beginning to contend that the pendulum has moved too far in the other direction and that some of the benefits of breast-feeding are being oversold. Is it any wonder that families are often slow to adjust to the winds of medical advice? Frequently, today's stupid, irresponsible, or overprotective family was yesterday's informed, intelligent consumer of medical information.

Sometimes the process of mutual labeling and misunderstanding, coupled with the physician's sense of overresponsibility and the presence of psychosocial problems in the patient and family, can lead to strangely escalating problems. In an interesting article titled "Physician-Patient Power Struggles: Their Role in Noncompliance," the family therapists Joellyn Ross and Etienne Phipps (1986) describe the circular power dynamics that can occur between physicians and "noncompliant" patients. They point out that when the patient does not get better, the physician can feel inadequate and vulnerable to self-doubt. The natural response for the physician is to escalate efforts to manage the disease and to get the patient to comply. The patient responds to this aggressive control effort by exerting countercontrol, which is most easily done by not complying and not getting better. After recounting a characteristic case, Ross and Phipps (1986, p. 100) describe the unfolding scene in this way:

> The physician and patient were involved in an "incongruous hierarchy," in which the patient's noncompliance served to maintain a balance of power between physician and patient. Each attempted to control the other by struggling to control the symptom. The patient was in a subordinate position by having an uncontrolled medical problem, and simultaneously in a superior position by not wishing to comply. The physician was in a superior position because of his/her professional role, but the patient's not complying rendered the physician ineffectual and subordinate. . . . Paradoxically, in order to be in control, the patient had to be out of control vis à vis the medical problem. If the patient were to comply and get better, the struggle would end and with this the partnership would have to change. Sometimes in these situations the physician becomes hopelessly frustrated, withdraws, and refers the patient elsewhere. Or, the patient becomes frustrated and changes physicians or drops out of treatment.

From complex, torturous situations such as this to simpler missteps in the dance between clinician and patient, the clash of explanatory models is one of the most difficult aspects of health care. If the clinician's ability to appraise illness symptoms based on scientific criteria were not valued in our culture, then people would not frequent health care professionals. Clearly, most patients and families want to benefit from the expertise of clinicians. And most clinicians want to be genuinely helpful within the limits of their training. A central difficulty lies with health care training, which traditionally has emphasized the biomedical aspects of health care to the neglect of the psychosocial aspects. Although nursing, family medicine, and pediatrics have made strides to a more biopsychosocial approach in their training programs in the past decade, we believe that most currently practicing clinicians lack ways to handle the clash of explanatory models in a constructive fashion.

IMPLICATIONS FOR
HEALTH PROFESSIONALS

Appreciating the importance of family health appraisal in clinical practice opens the door to rich information for the clinician and new approaches to patient care. Perhaps the most crucial challenge for most clinicians is to accept the social nature of diagnosis. Diagnosis is not just an activity inside the clinician's head. Diagnosis, as Glenn (1984) has pointed out, is a *social contract* involving the clinician, the patient, the family, other clinicians, and often a wider social network. A medical diagnosis is a "shared opinion" rather than a statement about objective reality. If this statement seems radical, consider how the content of diagnostic categories and the procedures for making diagnoses have changed drastically over the centuries, but diagnosis as a shared meaning between clinicians and patients has persisted. Without a common ground of shared opinion about the nature of health problems, long-term cooperation between clinicians and clients is unlikely to occur. In Glenn's (1984, p. 112) words concerning the clinician/patient relationship:

> Unless there is some kind of agreement, each of them is dancing in his own world, with his own ideas of what is wrong and what it signifies. Their activity is not coordinated. Further, without a mutual contract each is likely to misunderstand the other's intent and thoughts, and their relationship is jeopardized. The failure to establish an overt contract can lead to covert conflict.

After the clinician has grasped the social nature of the diagnostic process, the next clinical challenges are to develop skills in eliciting information about the patient's and family's explanatory models for health and illness, and skills in negotiating a shared meaning about the problem. Because many patients and family members are reluctant to appear ignorant in front of their health care provider, they are apt to keep quiet about their own explanations for their health problems. They then passively assent to the clinician's proffered diagnosis, while not really buying it. Therefore, the clinician needs ways of encouraging patients and families to discuss their health appraisals without fear of reproach. The family physicians Robert Like and R. Prasaad Steiner (1986, p. 90) offer the following questions that can help the clinician elicit explanatory models from patients. These questions are not so much a guide for every clinical interview as they are a set of sensitizing issues that can be explored with patients whose health beliefs appear to differ markedly from their clinician's.

(1) What do you call your problem? What name does it have?
(2) What do you think has caused your problem?
(3) Why do you think it started when it did?
(4) What does your sickness do to you? How does it work?
(5) How severe is it? Will it have a short or long course?
(6) What do you fear most about your sickness?
(7) What are the chief problems your sickness has caused you?
(8) What kind of treatment do you think you should receive? What are the most important results you hope to receive from your treatment?

To this list of questions we would add the following that relate to the family and the family health expert:

(9) Who have you talked with in your family about your problem?
(10) Is there someone in your family or close circle of friends whom you most often consult about your health concerns?
(11) What are that person's and other family members' opinions about what is wrong with you?
(12) What do they think should be done about it?
(13) Has anyone else among your family and friends had this kind of problem? What was the outcome for them?

In addition to questions such as these asked of the individual patient, the clinician may sometimes choose to call a family conference for the purpose of eliciting family health beliefs more directly. In either case, the clinician must be genuinely interested in exploring and acknowledging the family's understanding of the problem. Impatient or patronizing responses will lead either to no useful information or to a pitched battle between the clinician and the family. Families generally win such battles in the long run, because they must protect their own integrity.

After the clinician has come to understand the patient's, and accept the family's, understanding of the problem, a negotiating process can occur to develop a common agreement about diagnosis and treatment. This process can be particularly challenging for physicians who have been trained in the main political tenant of the biomedical model, namely, that the doctor *prescribes* and the patient *complies* (Doherty, Baird, & Becker, 1987). Experienced clinicians, however, often learn to seek a compromise that will allow the therapeutic relationship to continue rather than insisting that a resistant family immediately accept a medical diagnosis they find confusing or contradictory to their own beliefs. Many examples of this accommodation process appear in the cases presented in Doherty and Baird (1987).

To return to the first case illustration in this chapter—in which the parents were distraught about their daughter's low fever and mild sore throat—Dr. Crosby, after eliciting the family's explanatory model for their daughter's problem, could have negotiated with the parents in the following way: He begins by respectfully acknowledging and accepting their urgent fears, particularly because they have seen bad outcomes in their family from symptoms that began in the same manner. Dr. Crosby then gently restates his own belief that their daughter is probably not in trouble medically, and explain why he does not believe that she has meningitis. He offers to order laboratory tests if the parents feel that they cannot live with the doctor's assessment, but expresses his belief that the tests would be expensive and unproductive at this point. If the parents are willing to wait and monitor the child for the next day, however, Dr. Crosby and the parents can agree on the criteria for a serious "worsening" of her condition, such as a stiff neck or difficulty breathing. If those symptoms were to occur, Dr. Crosby promises to see the child quickly. And if the currently mild symptoms do not clear up in three days, Dr. Crosby will see the child in the office for further evaluation.

The outcome of this negotiated diagnostic process would likely be a healthy child and a collaborative clinician/family relationship. In collaboratively negotiating the diagnosis and treatment plan, the physician was actually "treating" the major problem: the parents' anxiety. Anxiety only rarely responds to rational explanations that do not offer emotional support. Dr. Crosby did not tell the parents that they were wrong, only that in his best judgment the child was not seriously ill. By proposing an agreement about further monitoring, however, Dr.

Crosby was implicitly accepting the possibility that the parents were correct. The compromise position was to wait and see if the doctor or the parents were correct, rather than engaging in further diagnostic work now. Both the clinician and the parents could feel respected in this process.

In cases in which the clinician is proposing a diagnosis that the patient and family reject, as in the case of the man with hypertension, described above, then negotiation can begin with the clinician accepting the patient's and family's right to disagree with the proffered medical diagnosis. Generally, a diagnosis carries with it a series of predictions about how the disease will progress. The clinician can attempt to negotiate with the patient and family a shared agreement that *if* the symptoms persist or develop in the manner suggested by the clinician's diagnosis, then that diagnosis is probably accurate. For example, if the diagnosis of moderate to severe hypertension is correct, then one would expect the patient's blood pressure to remain elevated consistently over a number of weeks or months. If the one-time reading was an aberration, then the blood pressure should not show consistently high readings over weeks and months. The clinician, patient, and family could agree in advance that two months of elevated readings would clinch the diagnosis of hypertension. By not rejecting the patient and family who disagree with a medically "straightforward" diagnosis, the clinician can keep the door open to an eventual shared meaning about the problem and its treatment.

In their article on teaching clinicians about cross-cultural health care, behavioral scientist Elois Berlin and family physician William Fowkes (1983, p. 934) nicely summarize several useful guidelines in the form of the acronym *LEARN*:

L   *Listen* with sympathy and understanding to the patient's perception of the problem.
E   *Explain* your perceptions of the problem.
A   *Acknowledge* and discuss the differences and similarities.
R   *Recommend* treatment.
N   *Negotiate* agreement.

Berlin and Fowkes point out that cultural and subcultural differences among patients prevent any clinician from becoming expert about the whole range of health beliefs that patients and families bring to the clinical encounter of medical care. Sensitivity to cultural differences and willingness to talk in depth about health beliefs with patients and families—these characteristics are more important for clinicians than an advanced understanding of medical anthropology. The patients and families will do the necessary teaching if the clinician is willing to learn.

CONCLUSION

Families appraise the health and illness of family members with a special blend of heart, mind, and history. Their appraisals no doubt reflect what David Reiss (1981) terms "family paradigms" concerning how the family relates to its social and physical environment. In their historical continuity and shared memories over generations, families transcend individual clinicians and the current state of medical knowledge. In truth, families care more about the health of their members than clinicians ever can. Their health appraisals, therefore, are more than reflections of "lay" understandings or misunderstandings about medical facts. These appraisals are ways that families give meaning to family life, keep alive the memories and influence of previous generations, protect the welfare of current family members, and negotiate diagnoses and treatments with the sometimes alien culture of the health care system. This unending family process offers a fascinating area of research for scholars and a challenging dimension of health care for clinicians.

DISCUSSION QUESTIONS

(1) What are your reactions to Dr. Crosby in the case illustrations? How typical are these vignettes of how physicians deal with family health beliefs?
(2) Can you identify a "family health expert" in your family of origin? Who was that person and how did he or she exercise the role?
(3) Take a disease and generate a list of common family health beliefs about it—beliefs not necessarily grounded in medical science. How are families with these beliefs likely to interact with health professionals?

RECOMMENDED READINGS

Glenn, M. L. (1984). *On diagnosis: A systemic approach.* New York: Brunner/Mazel.
Kleinman, A. (1980). *Patients and healers in the context of culture.* Berkeley: University of California Press.
Ross, J. L., & Phipps, E. (1986). Physician-patient power struggles: Their role in non-compliance. *Family Medicine, 18,* 99-101.

CHAPTER
5

Families' Acute Response to Illness

THE ONSET OF SERIOUS ILLNESS is one of the most feared and disruptive experiences in family life. Most adults have experienced the dreaded phone call telling of a family member's heart attack, emergency surgery, or diagnosis of cancer. Family reactions to the onset of serious illness, however, have been the least-studied domain of the family health and illness cycle. There are a number of good reasons for this gap. Families experiencing a health emergency are less willing to allow the intrusion of a research investigator than families who are in the long-term adjustment phase. Researchers for their part tend to be geared to studying established patients and families being treated at chronic illness clinics, rather than mobilizing research interviewers quickly when a diagnosis is newly made. Furthermore, researchers are concerned about adding to families' distress by interviewing them during the acute phase of an illness. For logistical and ethical reasons, then, researchers find it easier to study families after they have passed the acute phase of their reaction to an illness.

Research on the aftermath of the diagnosis of cancer is an important exception to this relative neglect of the acute phase of the family's response to illness. The rest of this chapter will deal with how families respond to the diagnosis and early treatment phases of cancer, and how health professionals interact with families during this stressful period.

CANCER IN AMERICAN LIFE

Cancer is the second leading cause of death in the United States, and no doubt is the disease most dreaded by Americans (AIDS may soon provide competition for "most feared" status). The facts are striking: Nearly a third of Americans can expect to get cancer during their lives, and three out of four families will have a family member diagnosed with cancer (American Cancer Society, 1982).

Beyond these epidemiological data, cancer has acquired a powerful cultural image in the Western world. In a chapter on changing attitudes toward death in Western society, the social historian Phillipe Aries (1975, pp. 140-141) writes:

> In our world where everyone acts as though medicine is the answer to everything . . . incurable diseases, particularly cancer, have taken on the hideous, terrifying aspects of the old representations of death. More than the skeleton or mummy of the *Macabres* of the 14th and 15th centuries, more than the leper with his bell, cancer today is death.

Although heart disease kills many more people in our country than cancer does, it is cancer that stirs our greatest fears. In an article on the cultural metaphor of cancer, Ellen Golub (1981) argues that cancer is experienced as our body turning uncontrollably against itself. Once unleashed, it often can be contained, if not cured, by technology that also renders the victim out of control. In Golub's (1981, p. 730) colorful language, "The cancer patient, host to a parasite gone wild in its development, is yoked to machine for detection and treatment and provokes in us our deepest dread and our darkest dreams."

These quotations capture the dual image of cancer for most American families: fear of death and fear of dependence on destructive technology for treatment. Until they experience cancer, families are less aware of the confusing and disruptive influences that cancer brings to family relationships. Ironically, this familial disruption by cancer may be increasing precisely because of improved treatment technology. From their experience at the University of Massachusetts Medical School, the team of Krant, Doster, and Ploof (1980, p. 54) write: "People now tend to live longer, undergo many more treatments, and find their lives in more chronic derangement. . . . Good medical care keeps people alive longer; confusing social responsibility and family relationships, however, take a different sort of toll." We turn now to this toll.

FAMILIES' REACTIONS TO CANCER

In this section, we review the findings of several representative studies on families' responses during the first months after the diagnosis of cancer in a family member.

The nursing researchers Marilyn Oberst and Ruth James (1985) were interested in the pattern of crisis development experienced by patient and spouse immediately after surgery for bowel and genitourinary cancer. Using an unstructured interview that was then coded for major concerns, coping strategies, and other coping issues, the investigators first spoke with the subjects at 1 to 2 days before discharge from the hospital after surgery, followed by interviews at 10, 30, and 60 days after discharge. Forty patients and spouses were interviewed on these four occasions, while a subset of 26 couples also were interviewed 90 and 180 days after discharge.

The authors found major changes over time in the patients' and spouses' concerns and stressors. During the hospitalization period, spouses reported symptoms of fatigue and anorexia (loss of appetite), and feelings of shock and the need to be cheerful for the patient. Interestingly, the spouse's level of anxiety was higher than the patient's during this period. During the first 30 days after surgery, both were concerned primarily with the patient's physical health; other personal and marital concerns were put on "hold." After the 30-day period, spouses also became concerned about their own health and with the impact of the cancer on their own lives.

By two months, spouses in this study were expressing increasing anger and resentment about the disruption caused by the disease. They reported fatigue; multiple physical problems such as aches, pains, indigestion, and exacerbation of preexisting conditions; and upper respiratory tract infections. Significantly, patients consistently reported less distress than spouses did, and showed little awareness of their spouses' worry and distress. As one spouse expressed, "He has the cancer—I'm not sick, so I'm not allowed to have a bad day" (Oberst & James, 1985, p. 52). The spouses felt that they got back little in return for their support, either from the patient or from outside sources. By six months, most patients were back to work, and disruptions of family life related to the disease were reported only when there was recurrence of the cancer or complications of further treatment. The spouses' feelings of depression and anger remained, however, along with guilt for having these feelings and for wanting to take care of their own needs. The

Oberst and James (1985) investigation attests to the significant stress experienced by the caretaking family member during the period following cancer surgery.

Studies over the years have differed in their assessments of the impact of childhood cancer on marriage. While several uncontrolled studies found high marital disruption rates for these couples, the pediatrician Shirley Lansky and her colleagues (1978) at the University of Kansas reported that the divorce rate in a sample of 191 parents was not higher than the comparable regional divorce rate. The authors did find, however, that, on a measure of marital distress, cancer parents rated themselves as more troubled than a normal control group and a control group of hemophilia parents, but less troubled than a marriage counseling group.

Similar good new/bad news findings were reported by the psychologist Oscar Barbarin and his colleagues (1985) in a study of couples with children who had cancer. The majority of the 32 couples reported that their marital and family cohesion was strengthened by their experience with childhood cancer and that their spouse was their main source of support. The authors found, however, that the more hospitalizations the child experienced, the lower the reported marital support and marital quality. Of particular importance in maintaining or declining marital quality for wives was their perception of their husbands' involvement in the care of the child. For husbands, the key issue was their perception of their wives' availability in the home as opposed to the hospital.

Unlike most studies that focus on the impact of the stress of cancer on marital relationships, the Canadian behavioral scientists Ilze Kalnins, M. Pamela Churchill, and Grace Terry (1980) examined the *additional* stressors being experienced by cancer families in the rest of their lives. The researchers followed 45 families with a leukemic child for 20 months after the diagnosis. After each formal research interview was completed, the investigators engaged families in informal discussion and took field notes about what families volunteered about significant family life events. Given that families were not asked specifically about stressful events, the authors point out that the findings probably underestimate what was going on with their sample of Toronto families representing a wide range of socioeconomic groups. The list of concurrent stresses for these families was impressive. The percentages below reflect the number of families volunteering information on the concurrent stressor.

— Noncancer medical complications in the child: 27%
— Death of another leukemic child not in the family: 35%
— Death of another significant person: 13%
— Serious concurrent illness in a family member: 44%
— Occupational changes: 22%
— Financial problems: 13%
— Miscellaneous (moving, vacation, marriage, auto accidents): 40%

Overall, 14 families had four or more significant life events, and 26 families had one to three life events. Only 5 families failed to volunteer an important life event over the 20-month period. Because this study does not report on comparative life events of a control group, the results must be taken with caution. The study suggests, however, the twin possibilities that the family's response to cancer will be affected by the concurrent stressors occurring in the family's life, and that the experience of coping with cancer will affect the likelihood that the family will experience further major stressful events.

The family social scientist Alberta Koch's (1985) investigation of pediatric cancer families supports the findings of the other studies cited in this discussion. She interviewed siblings and parents of 32 randomly selected pediatric cancer patients who had been diagnosed from 6 to 36 months before. Koch asked respondents directly about personal and familial changes following the diagnosis of cancer up until the present time. Analysis of the interviews indicated that 14 of the families had implicit rules prohibiting emotional expression, especially of worry and anger. This form of family repression or denial appeared to stifle emotional contact. As in the Kalnins et al. (1980) study, about three-fourths of the families showed a pileup of other stressors, particularly health problems and psychosocial problems. About two-thirds of the mothers reported feeling emotionally abandoned by other adult family members for varying amounts of time after the diagnosis. Half of the families showed a patient-centered role configuration—focusing most family concern on the sick child—that led siblings to feel left out. Koch's study suggests the importance of family rules concerning emotional expression and of the family's ability to shift roles so that mothers and siblings receive support and attention.

In summary, the literature on families and cancer indicates that in the early, postdiagnosis phase of cancer, many families experience shock and disbelief. Their energies during the initial period are focused on the physical survival of the cancer patient. Family members, particularly

spouses and mothers, experience much fatigue during the hospitalization period. Once the acute crisis phase is over, families differ in how
they handle the initial adjustment to living with cancer and its treatment.
A common experience is for the wife/mother to assume the major
responsibility for caretaking, and for her to feel emotionally and
physically unsupported by her husband and the extended family. In
addition, some families focus on the ill member to the detriment of the
needs of other family members, especially siblings of child cancer
patients. Many families have difficulty communicating openly with one
another about their intense feelings of fear, worry, anger, and resentment. These problems notwithstanding, some families appear to
become more cohesive and satisfied with their family ties through
coping with the experience of cancer.

CASE ILLUSTRATION:
"A CANCER PATIENT AND HIS
FAMILY FACE THE FUTURE"[1]

by Craig Peters

Last Spring, I underwent surgery to remove a rapidly growing tumor
from the side of my head. Five days later pathology reports were
complete. My family physician came by in the afternoon but I was home
for supper, thanks to a four hour pass from the hospital. At 9:30 that
evening, after an outing with his daughter, he came back. He began,
"Well, the path reports were not what we wanted and hoped for ..." and
went on from there to speak of angiosarcoma, a rarely seen but
apparently virile form of cancer, about which little was known at that
point by any of the local physicians involved. Treatment was uncertain.
Further surgery and other forms of treatment might be recommended.
There were no promises. As might be expected, my hopes crashed and
my heart broke. I felt empty inside and cried as he went on. I had not
really expected the news, even though I knew it was possible and had
done some work in anticipation of what it would mean to get that report.
The news itself, however, knocked me out emotionally.

The doctor paused and waited in the dark silence with me. He
wondered how I'd like this news to be shared with my wife and family.
Instantly, I knew what had to happen. Without a moment's hesitation

and with an assertiveness that surprised me I said, "Doctor, I am going to ask you to drive me home right now. My parents, my wife, my children are all there. I'd like you to share with them, just as you have with me, the whole story." He agreed at once. I went on, "And one more thing. I don't want us to spend this night alone. We need to face this together, so I want you to check me out for the night, let me sleep at home, and I'll be back whenever you need me here in the morning."

The second request was more difficult for him. He agreed fully with the process but knew, more than I did, the administrative issues it might raise. Noting that, he said he'd go to work on it and be back in a few minutes. While I cried, prayed, and sat with my roommate watching the full moon, a great quiet came over me. Meanwhile, the doctor went through various levels of administration to clear the way.

Soon we were in his car. At home, I went in with the doctor and called the family together. We sat holding each other as he went over the story, again sharing openly what he knew and didn't know, making special efforts to include my daughters, inviting and responding to their questions, and quietly acknowledging our feelings. One daughter asked if it was hereditary, and he explained he didn't know for this type of cancer, but would attempt to find out more and would let her know. A couple of times there was silence and I thought we were done, but the doctor did not run away from the intensity of the moment. He sat with us till he was sure we needed no more from him. It was about 11:00 pm when he left. We talked, cried, held each other, and phoned a few close friends. I spent a few minutes with everybody before we were all tired out and went to bed. Each person slept surprisingly well.

I only began to realize how unconventional my requests and his response had been, when over the next few days, nurses, supervisors and other physicians came by to talk about this unusual event. What seemed new was the inclusion of children and, in this case, grandparents, from the very beginning, in the realities of the situation. The flexibility of this physician and hospital to adapt structures and normal procedures in order to meet the immediate human need was also noteworthy. He calls it "just listening to your own human responses, doing what makes sense and feels right." He believes that major illness is a family emergency in which each member has a concern and to which each one must respond.

At that stage my family needed good information about what was happening and could be expected ahead. We needed time to process that information alone and then with others, including the doctor. Soon the need shifted to emotional support, since my wife and children faced feelings comparable to my own: shock, disbelief, anger, fear, sadness, helplessness, hope, confusion and much more. We all needed help to acknowledge and express some of these feelings to ourselves, and to others, in functional rather than dysfunctional ways.

My physician followed through his family oriented approach in several ways over the next few months. He made special efforts to answer my daughter's request for information about heredity and this type of cancer. He spoke with her personally about the information he had uncovered, which was very important to her since 30 years ago my mother died of an unidentified form of cancer at just my age. In his many contacts with me throughout the summer and fall he consistently inquired about how various members of the family were doing.

He kept in touch with other family members too. He used a routine office visit to involve my daughters in a discussion of how things were going at home, how the family was having to adjust, and especially how all of this was affecting them. He invited my wife and me to couple sessions in which we moved from the medical concerns around treatments and the advancing cancer to personal concerns and couple issues which might be arising. In the Fall he arranged to meet the family in our home, to explore individual and family responses to the situation and to each other during this time. Some important work was done in this meeting, acknowledging anger and frustration at the disruption cancer was causing in all of our lives, as well as our fears about our futures, since it was becoming quite clear that I would probably not recover and the road ahead would not likely be any better—it was just unknown.

I have written this to express deep appreciation to my physician. I also want to encourage others who recognize that major illness is a family affair because of its impact on each member of the family and the system as a whole. They too are in stress and in need of support during times of family crisis; the unit of treatment is the whole family.

I am a pastoral counselor and a marriage and family therapist. I tend to see things from a family systems perspective. Through this experience, however, I am no objective observer or researcher—I am pure patient, trembling and struggling with all that is happening to me and to my family.

FAMILIES' INTERACTIONS WITH HEALTH PROFESSIONALS DURING THE ACUTE PHASES OF CANCER

As Craig Peters's story so beautifully illustrates, health care interactions around serious illness occur within the triangle of the patient, the family, and a clinician. In the case of the diagnosis of cancer, all three parts of what Doherty and Baird (1983) call the "therapeutic triangle"—including the clinician—are stressed. Primary care physicians in particular often experience two kinds of dread related to cancer: one involving finding cancer in a patient whom the physician knows and cares about, and the other involving missing an early diagnosis that could save the patient's life. Thus the doctor may be fearful of looking for cancer, and fearful of not looking for it.

Only rarely does a primary care physician make a definitive diagnosis of cancer. Usually this task is the responsibility of a specialist such as an oncologist in a hospital setting. Once the diagnosis is made, two important interactions occur between the clinicians and the patient and family: informing of the diagnosis and making decisions concerning treatment. These seemingly straightforward processes are in fact quite treacherous. The primary care physician may be feeling guilty about not picking up the diagnosis sooner, the oncologist does not know the patient and family and may be primarily oriented to the technological aspects of cancer treatment, and the patient and family naturally are very anxious about the future. Furthermore, in tertiary care medical centers where many cancer patients are diagnosed and treated, there will be a variety of other resident physicians and nurses involved in the case, and the patient and family may be asked immediately to decide whether to participate in a research protocol. Clearly, there is a lot happening quickly once a diagnosis of cancer is made.

The internist psychiatrist Melvin Krant and his psychologist colleague Lee Johnston have provided interesting documentation of these interactions between medical staff and families (Krant & Johnston, 1978). They interviewed 75 patients and 126 family members about their experiences with the medical staff during different phases of cancer treatment. The patients were in three medical oncology units at two hospitals, one public and one private, in New England. In all, 60% of the patients and 33% of the family members reported that they were not initially clearly informed of the cancer diagnosis. The rest were told that there was a "tumor" or something vague. Of the family members, 15%

were angry about how they were told the diagnosis, and only 33% felt that a physician had been helpful to them during the course of the cancer treatment. Krant and Johnston (1977-1978, p. 212) summarize some of their findings as follows:

> Close family members indicate that they frequently learn of a patient's diagnosis through a non-medical source, many indicate that they do not know the name of the present physician caring for the patient, and many do little or no talking with the physicians, and therefore, not surprisingly, do not find the physicians helpful to them for their problems relating to the patient's illness. In those instances wherein the family member did not establish communication with the physician at the time of diagnosis, almost invariably that person did not feel that he could communicate with the subsequent physicians from that point on.

In fairness to the physicians in this study, we note that some patients and families deny the presence of cancer and thus may "forget" that the physicians told them the correct information. Our observation is that American physicians increasingly are informing patients—although this is less consistent for family members—about the diagnosis of cancer. These physicians tend to become caught up in the technical aspects of establishing a treatment protocol for the patient, however, leaving the family feeling excluded from the process. In her review of the impact of cancer on the family, nurse Laurel Northouse (1984) singled out "feeling excluded from the focus of care" as a major problem for family members during the initial phase of cancer treatment. The hospital is viewed by families as oriented primarily to the medical needs of the patient, with family members left to fend for themselves. Perhaps more serious, families also report feeling excluded from the crucial decisions about treatment protocols. As the technology of cancer treatment becomes more powerful, it also has become more potentially damaging to the rest of the patient's body and to the patient's morale. Failure to be consulted in these life and death decisions leaves many families feeling bereft and sometimes angry at the medical staff. The medical staff, for their part, often feel overwhelmed by biomedical demands and lack adequate training in communicating effectively with patients and families.

Much of the clinical and research literature on families' interactions with the health care team during cancer treatment has focused on the negative aspects of care. The psychiatrists George Marten and Alvin Mauer, for example, document the blaming and withdrawing that distressed health care professionals may engage in when dealing with cancer relapses. They (1982, p. 541) write that, when treatment is not going well, team members "may become irritable, verbally attack other team members, complain about the patient's parents, or withdraw entirely from the patient." Marten and Mauer suggest that the health care team sometimes needs therapy as much as the family does.

The psychologists Oscar Barbarin and Mark Chesler (1984), taking a more positive tack, decided to investigate factors that lead to satisfaction with care by parents of children with cancer. Using interviews and questionnaires with a sample of 74 parents at the University of Michigan Hospital, the authors found that parents' general satisfaction with the medical staff was most highly related to their amount of personal contacts with the physicians, especially their warmth, concern, and attention to the parents as individuals. Parents were most apt to feel supported by medical staff who kept them informed about the child's condition and who accepted the parents' competence in assisting with treatment and decision making. Overall, Barbarin and Chesler conclude that information transmission and personal contact were the strongest predictors of parents' satisfaction with the treatment their children were receiving at the institution.

In summary, there appear to be many problems with families' interactions with health care professionals during the early stages of cancer diagnosis and treatment. Families generally are dealing with unfamiliar health professionals with whom they have no common background experience, especially if the primary care physician backs out of the treatment picture. The medical team is oriented to implementing treatment protocols for the patient, and often has little time and training for thoroughly informing the family and giving them personal attention. Barbarin and Chesler's (1984) research suggests, however, that attention to these family issues leads families to evaluate positively the medical care that patients are receiving. Such attention may also forestall the family distress that accompanies the progression of cancer and the adjustment phase after initial treatment.

IMPLICATIONS FOR CLINICIANS

In Craig Peters's case illustration, the physician demonstrated the therapeutic power of dealing directly, informatively, and compassionately with a cancer patient and family. He demonstrated flexibility in modifying the hospital routine to accommodate the special needs of his patient. He met with the family, told them what he knew and didn't know, and "did not run away from the intensity of the moment." He continued with a family-oriented approach over the months that followed, attending to the unique needs of each family member and to the couple's and family's well-being. This physician "wrote the book" on caring for cancer patients and their families.

Following is a summary of specific implications for clinicians who work with the early stages of cancer treatment:

The stress that clinicians experience in diagnosing and treating cancer is exceeded only by the stress associated with suffering from cancer or having a family member suffering from cancer. The first implication for health professionals, then, is for them to make use of their own social supports. In working with cancer patients and families, the adage "Clinician, heal thyself" seems particularly appropriate. Difficulty in handling one's own emotions feeds into the institutional structures that depersonalize patients in hospitals. Sharing feelings and fears with other professionals, and with one's family and friends, can help the clinician to help the patient and family. It also is likely to improve working relationships in the health care team.

A second implication stems from the research and clinical experience testifying to families' desires for accurate information about the diagnosis and prognosis of cancer. It is too easy for uncomfortable clinicians to omit the words *cancer* and *malignancy* from their discussions with patients and families. On the one extreme is the clinician who talks vaguely about a tumor that will require further evaluation; on the other is the clinician who uses esoteric medical terms but does not spell out the diagnosis in terms the patient and family can understand. An in-between mistake is to tell the patient about the cancer but not meet with the family to tell them. Whatever misunderstandings or denials the patient experiences will then be passed on to the family. A conference with the patient and close family members may not be a pleasant task for the clinical team, but it is an essential one for beginning a cooperative therapeutic relationship. Doherty and Baird's (1987) casebook of family-centered medical care contains several examples of valuable conferences with cancer patients and their families.

A third implication concerns collaborative sharing of decisions about cancer treatment. Immediately upon receiving the shock of the cancer diagnosis, the patient and family are faced with decisions concerning treatment versus no treatment, and if treatment is initiated, what kind. For cancers where an effective treatment is available, such as many forms of childhood leukemia, the clinician's responsibility is to inform the patient and family about what to expect from the treatment regime, and to plan collaboratively the mechanics of scheduling and the parents' participation in the care. For cancers where treatment protocols are controversial, such as breast cancer where physicians differ on the use and extent of surgery, the clinician's first challenge is to inform the patient and family as clearly as possible about the available treatment options, without overwhelming them with the details of each treatment. The second challenge is genuinely to share the decision-making process with the patient and family by declining to fall back on "doctor's orders." For cancers such as liver cancer and metastatic brain tumors, for which debilitating chemotherapy may slightly prolong life while making that life very unpleasant, the clinical challenge is to allow the patient and family to make the entire decision about whether to proceed. Accepting a "no treatment" decision may be particularly difficult for physicians who are trained to go "all out" for every patient and for those who need patients for clinical research studies of new medications. Graciously and supportively accepting a patient's decision to die without medical intervention is a hallmark of a mature clinician.

A fourth implication relates to trying to understand the family's health beliefs related to cancer. As mentioned before, cancer has assumed a set of powerful cultural symbols and myths. Parents may assume that something they did or failed to do has caused their child's leukemia. Family members may believe that cancer is contagious. A family conference at the time of diagnosis can be used to elicit these health beliefs, to honor the feelings behind them, and, where appropriate, to try to substitute better information.

A fifth implication deals with helping patients and families with the psychological and social dynamics of cancer. By understanding the normal stresses experienced by families dealing with cancer, the clinician can perform two important functions: first, to educate families about the normal feelings they are experiencing and the normal strains that may lie ahead for them; and, second, to offer emotional support in the form of listening and touching.

Finally, an important task for clinicians who deal with cancer is to inform families about support groups and other community resources. The "I Can Cope" program is a national self-help group for cancer patients and family members. Some professionals conduct open enrollment groups that offer information and support. One such program is described by the social workers Edith Johnson and Doretta Stark (1980). For families who need far more intensive help, there are options for therapy such as the family group therapy program offered by the psychologist/nurse team of Wellisch, Mosher, and Van Scoy (1978) in a private oncology practice. Many communities offer such programs for cancer patients and their families. Supporting and educating families of cancer patients is too big a job for individual clinicians. A network of groups and treatment programs is crucial to the delivery of comprehensive care for cancer.

CONCLUSION

The diagnosis and early treatment of cancer present families with extraordinary demands and extraordinary opportunities. Research evidence and clinical experience attest to the difficulties families experience in maintaining their emotional equilibrium and mutual supportiveness in the wake of cancer's appearance in their lives. These difficulties frequently are not addressed by health professionals— themselves stressed—who focus on the biomedical aspects of the disease. On the other hand, some families experience renewed bonds of closeness through dealing with this emergency. When a hurting family such as Craig Peters's in the case illustration is fortunate enough to encounter a caring and collaborative clinician, both parties are enriched and ennobled by their joint struggle. Cancer in our culture is a crucible upon which families and clinicians alike become enabled or disabled.

DISCUSSION QUESTIONS

(1) Recall a sudden onset of a serious illness in your nuclear family or extended family. How did your family react? Did any of the research findings summarized in this chapter fit your family's experience?

(2) Why do you think cancer is such a uniquely feared disease in American society? Why is it harder for people to admit they have cancer than to admit to lung disease or heart disease? How do these issues affect how families deal with cancer?

(3) Why is cancer so difficult for clinicians to cope with? How could health

care institutions be changed to help clinicians cope better and work better with cancer patients and families?

RECOMMENDED READINGS

Barbarin, O. A., & Chesler, M. A. (1984). Relationships with the medical staff and aspects of satisfaction with care expressed by parents of children with cancer. *Journal of Community Health, 9,* 302-313.

Lewis, F. M. (1986). The impact of cancer on the family: A critical analysis of the research literature. *Patient Education and Counseling,* [no volume no.], pp. 269-289.

Schulman, J. L., & Kupst, M. J. (1980). *The child with cancer.* Springfield, IL: Charles C Thomas.

NOTE

1. The source of this case illustration is as follows: Peters, C., A cancer patient and his family face the future. *Can Fam Physician* 1985; 31:1177-8. Reprinted by permission.

The author, Craig Peters, who was from Kitchener, Ontario, Canada, died shortly after this article was accepted for publication.

CHAPTER

6

Family
Adaptation
to Illness
and Recovery

Life is not a matter of holding good cards, but of playing a poor hand well.

Robert Louis Stevenson
(who suffered from tuberculosis)

CHRONIC ILLNESS is a nearly universal part of the life course of families. Half of all people over age 65 and one-fourth of people between ages 45 and 65 are limited in their activities by at least one chronic condition (U.S. Department of Commerce, 1980). As documented previously in this volume, chronic disease is increasing in prevalence, replacing acute disease as the leading cause of morbidity and mortality in the United States. As Thomas Campbell (1986) points out in his review of the impact of families on health and illness, the experience of chronic illness affects family life in profound ways, and the way the family handles chronic illness can strongly influence the course of the illness itself.

Most research on families and chronic illness has studied the psychological impact on other family members. For example, there are many studies looking at the effects of childhood illnesses on mothers and siblings (Breslau et al., 1981, 1982; Cairns et al., 1979; Lavigne & Ryan, 1979). As important as it is to study the psychosocial impact of chronic illness, we believe this one-directional approach (i.e., illness affects family members) fails to capture the complexities of the *interactions* between families and chronic illness. In this chapter, we will use a biopsychosocial, or systems, approach that assumes reciprocal interactions and influence among the family, the individual, and the illness. An orienting question is as follows: "How does the family organize itself around chronic illness?" We will use diabetes as a chief example, because diabetes is a widespread, serious chronic disease about which much family-oriented research has been published. We will also discuss interchanges between health professionals and families around chronic illness, and offer some suggestions for clinicians caring for families with a chronically ill member.

We organize our literature review and discussion of the family factors in chronic illness around the Family FIRO model developed by William Doherty and his colleague Nicholas Colangelo (Doherty & Colangelo, 1984). The model is derived from the Fundamental Inter-personal Relations Orientation (FIRO) model of pioneering group theorist Will Schutz (1958), which Doherty and Colangelo have applied to the family field. Briefly, the Family FIRO model proposes that relationship patterns in families and other social groups can be categorized into issues of *inclusion* (belonging, role patterns, bound-aries), *control* (influence, power, conflict), and *intimacy* (close personal exchanges, in-depth sharing, "I-Thou" relations). Theoretically, any ongoing behavior pattern in a family can be viewed as serving to achieve, maintain, or modify some aspect of inclusion, control, or intimacy in family relationships. Doherty and Whitehead (1986) have used this model to analyze the social dynamics of cigarette smoking. For example, they view smoking as a way that some couples are bonded by a shared, unpopular habit, and as a way that some spouses exclude themselves when family members disapprove of their smoking (inclusion issues). Smoking is frequently the subject of power struggles in families as family members try to persuade a recalcitrant smoker to quit (control issue). And smoking and sexual intimacy have long been linked culturally in our society (intimacy issue).

Using the Family FIRO model, we will examine family interactions around chronic illness according to dimensions of family inclusion, family control, and family intimacy. The following case illustration shows the way a couple has dealt with these issues surrounding the wife's rheumatoid arthritis. Inclusion is seen in their efforts to redefine their roles and their common activities; control, in their conflicts about the illness; and intimacy, in their greater closeness through dealing honestly with their feelings. The subsequent presentation in the chapter will be based upon research findings and our clinical experience in caring for these families.

CASE ILLUSTRATION 1

Jill was a very active and athletic woman until she began developing knee pain and stiffness at the age of 22. The pain gradually worsened and spread to other joints over the next two years, when the diagnosis of rheumatoid arthritis was made. Despite medical treatment, she became increasingly disabled and dependent on crutches for walking. Over the next five years, she had several joint replacements with some improvement in her mobility and pain. Her disabilities and frequent hospitalizations, however, forced her to drop out of her master's degree program in education, and at age 30 she began part-time work teaching children with learning disabilities.

Jill's husband Steve was a workaholic and the only child of emotionally distant parents. As Jill's disease progressed, roles and responsibilities that had developed over their 10-year marriage had to be renegotiated. Steve assumed more responsibilities at home and shifted his energies from his busy law practice to the care of their five-year-old daughter, Annie. He became involved in the PTA and other school activities. Despite Jill's disabilities, she continued to do the cooking for the family, and shared in the parenting. Simple daily tasks that had been taken for granted now required careful planning. No longer able to share outdoor recreation, the couple was forced to search for new common activities.

Jill and Steve are at different stages in dealing with the illness. Steve has not fully accepted Jill's diagnosis, and continues to search for a cure. He struggles with his anger toward his wife for being ill, her physicians for failing to cure her, and the illness for its effects on their family. Jill is grieving over the loss of her former health, and is attempting to reorganize her life around her limited physical abilities. As a couple, they go through periods of intense conflict, with each feeling resentful of the other.

Working through these conflicts and learning to share their feelings about the changes in their lives, in addition to their success in making positive adjustments in their daily lives, has brought them closer together emotionally than at any time during their marriage.

INCLUSION IN FAMILIES WITH
CHRONIC ILLNESS

The family psychiatrist Peter Steinglass and his colleagues (1982) have demonstrated how families tend to pull together during the acute phases of an illness in order to protect the ill family member from harm (see also Maurin & Schenkel, 1976). Families are especially likely to become more cohesive and integrated in the face of illnesses of sudden onset that are incapacitating or potentially fatal. If the family member survives, the initial series of cohesive interactions face the test of the chronic stage of the illness experience. Two extreme reactions are possible. On the one hand, the family may remain tightly bound together, focused on the illness, but impeding the ill member's autonomy and responsibility for self-care. On the other hand, the family may pull apart, with the ill member or another family member completely disengaging from the family. Where the family settles between these two extremes of inclusion will depend upon the preillness functioning of the family, the stage of the family life cycle, and psychosocial characteristics of the illness itself (Rolland, 1984).

A number of studies have documented the increased interpersonal distance that some families create when coping with chronic, incapacitating illness. Some families are not able to tolerate the physical and emotional demands of these illnesses. They, therefore, distance themselves from the illness and, in some cases, even exclude the ill family member. A common example occurs when a family, overburdened by the demands of caring for a demented parent at home, decides to put him or her in a nursing home. Isaacs (1971) has demonstrated that the family's perception of the burden is the best predictor of whether the elderly family member is placed in an institution. Marital disruption and divorce may be other forms of exclusion. Spouses of chronically ill patients may be unable or unwilling to cope with the changes in the marital relationship that inevitably occur with chronic illness. They may have as much subjective distress as the chronically ill spouse (Cassileth et al., 1985; Klein, 1967). Overall, studies have shown an increase in marital distress, but not in divorce, among families with chronically ill children (Sabbeth & Leventhal, 1984).

When a chronic illness is terminal, the famiy may gradually exclude the dying family member before death, as a form of anticipatory grieving and to protect the rest of the family. The family psychiatrist David Reiss and his colleagues (1986), in their study of families with members who have end-stage renal disease (a terminal stage of kidney disease), found that *healthy* family functioning was associated with *early* death from kidney failure. The researchers speculated that these well-functioning families excluded the ill member as a last-stage coping effort, and that the ill member accepted early death as a way to help preserve the integrity of the family.

Frequently, the inclusion patterns associated with chronic illness are different for different parts of the family. Chronic illness can lead to increased closeness between some members of a family and distance or exclusion of others. Family therapists at the Chronic Illness Project at the Ackerman Institute of Family Therapy (Penn, 1983; Walker, 1983) and at the Philadelphia Child Guidance Clinic (Sargent, 1983) have described cross-generational coalitions (one parent allied with a child against the other parent) that occur in some families with chronic illness. The most common coalition involves a close bond between the chronically ill child and the caretaking mother, with a correspondingly weak bond between both of them and the father. The father remains disengaged from the family and the illness (Binger et al., 1969). Similar cross-generational alliances can be observed in families caring for an elderly parent at home. For example, the middle-aged daughter may become enmeshed with her elderly mother or father, with her husband preoccupying himself with his work. Unlike the *covert* cross-generational coalitions that have been described by the family therapist Jay Haley (1980), coalitions in families with chronic illness frequently are acknowledged and accepted by the family and outsiders as necessary to cope with the illness. Moreover, these patterns may reflect similar dynamics in how previous generations coped with chronic illness. Although accepted by the family and many health professionals as normal and inevitable, cross-generational coalitions may overburden the principal caretaker, diminish marital intimacy, and prevent the family from using their collective resources to cope with the illness.

Family Inclusion and the
Family Life Cycle

Just as chronic illness is not a static process, so too are families always changing and developing. Researchers and clinicians are only beginning to understand how changes in disease process and family process covary across time. A family with a diabetic preschooler will likely function differently than one with an adolescent diabetic or an elderly diabetic. Each of these families faces different developmental issues that are influenced by the illness. We have found family therapist Lee Combrinck-Graham's (1985) Developmental Model for Family Systems (Figure 6.1) particularly useful for understanding how the family life cycle and the chronic illness interact around issues of inclusion. In this model, the family system oscillates between periods of family closeness and family distance, and typically passes through three oscillations during a lifetime, one for each new generation. The periods of family closeness, such as childbirth, childbearing, and grandparent-hood, are called "centripetal" because the predominant forces are pulling the family together. The periods of family distance, such as adolescence, mid-life crisis, and retirement, are called "centrifugal" because the family is pulling apart. As the family psychiatrist John Rolland (1986) has observed, the direction a family is moving in its life cycle will have a profound influence on how it deals with a chronic illness.

If a chronic illness occurs when a family is in a centripetal phase of development, the additional inward pull of the illness may lead to *enmeshment*, a term used by Minuchin et al. (1975) to describe families in which members overreact to one another and discourage personal autonomy. This pattern has been described in families of young children with cerebral palsy (Schaffer, 1964) and epilepsy (Ritchie, 1981). Minuchin and colleagues (1975, 1978) have described an extreme form of this pattern in families of children with diabetes, asthma, and anorexia nervosa. These authors have demonstrated how this family pattern leads to worsening of the illness.

If a chronic illness occurs when a family is in a centrifugal period, such as adolescence, it may interfere with the family member's efforts to leave home and develop personal autonomy. Some incapacitating illnesses, such as spinal cord injuries, may physically prevent the adolescent from gaining independence. Other illnesses, such as diabetes, may intensify parent-child conflicts, especially over the child's autonomy in controlling the illness, thereby leading to exacerbation of the illness (Walker, 1983). In some families who are having difficulty loosening the emotional bonds of the family and letting children go, a chronic illness may give "permission" for the adolescent to remain dependent and at home. This pattern of interaction has been described by Jay Haley (1980) in schizophrenia and by the family therapists and

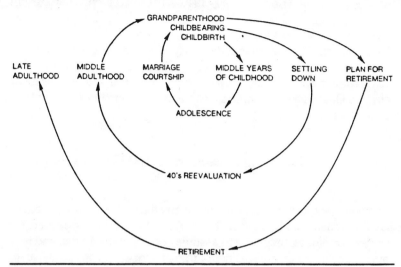

Figure 6.1 Family Life Spiral

SOURCE: Combrinck-Graham (1985). Reprinted by permission.

researchers M. Duncan Stanton and Thomas Todd (1982) in drug addiction.

Family Role Changes and Chronic Illness

When an illness is disabling, it requires a change in roles and task allocation within the family. If a parent in a two-parent family becomes incapacitated, the family functionally becomes a single-parent family with a new dependent family member. The healthy parent may try to assume all the parenting responsibilities or may share them with a grandparent, or with a child who becomes "parentified." Physical symptoms can develop in the healthy spouse who experiences severe role tension related to wearing too many "hats" in the family (Klein et al., 1967). If the ill person's previous role responsibilities are completely removed, he or she may feel unneeded and withdraw from the family (Bruhn, 1977). Role changes that minimize personal loss and offer other valuable contributions to the family may help preserve self-dignity and prevent "giving up." For example, disabled husbands who are unable to provide for the family economically may assume more responsibilities within the home (Komarovsky, 1940). These role changes are not necessarily determined by the amount of disability, but are strongly influenced by family dynamics (Cobb et al., 1969; Fink et al., 1968). The key family quality may be what the family researcher David Olson terms "family adaptability," the ability of the family to change its roles and rules to deal with challenges it faces (Olson et al., 1979). Disabling chronic illness provides families with a most severe challenge to their adaptability.

CONTROL IN FAMILIES WITH CHRONIC ILLNESS

Negotiating responsibility for managing the illness is the key control issue in families with chronic illness. As families coalesce around the crisis of an illness, they tend to assume control of the illness, and take over many of the responsibilities of the ill member. While this is usually adaptive in the acute phase, this process can lead to power struggles over the long run as the ill member tries to reassert control over his or her life. For example, families have been found to have lower expectations of children with chronic diseases, a situation that leads to both self-esteem and discipline problems in the children (Ferrari et al., 1983).

Noncompliance with medical regimens is often a sign of covert conflict over control. If the family has tried to assume control of a member through an illness, the only way the ill person can establish his or her own control is to resist the efforts of the family. This dynamics has been analyzed by the family therapists Paul Watzlawick and James Coyne (1980). The power struggle becomes overt in anorexia nervosa, when the adolescent refuses to eat, or vomits whatever is consumed. Control struggles have been linked to poor management of the chronic illness. For example, a harsh, authoritarian style of parenting and the frequent use of punishment have been found associated with poor control of childhood diabetes (Marrero et al., 1982) and epilepsy (Hauck, 1972).

Chronic illness itself may be a powerful regulator of family conflict. Minuchin et al. (1975) have described how childhood illness can be used to defuse parental conflict. The asthmatic child may begin to wheeze when parents fight, thereby diverting their energies. In couples in which there is a chronic illness, the illness itself may play an important role in regulating the relationship. Conflicts may be blamed on the illness, or the ill person may not be seen as responsible for his or her behavior because of the illness.

INTIMACY IN FAMILIES WITH CHRONIC ILLNESS

Changes in the level of intimacy in families with chronic illness depend upon family members' willingness and ability to share their feelings about the illness and the changes it has brought. Fear, anger, guilt, and depression are the most common emotions felt in these families. When there is significant denial of these uncomfortable feelings, a decrease in intimacy may result. Illness can lead to increased intimacy for families who face and share the experience of illness.

With every serious illness, there is fear about the future: Will the person recover, or become more disabled, or suffer more? How will the family cope? And often the most frightening question: Will the family member die? These can be extremely difficult issues for families to discuss, especially when the illness is disabling, progressive, or life threatening (Rolland, 1984). There can be secrecy concerning the prognosis of the illness, with family members covertly agreeing not to discuss it (Northouse, 1984). Families sometimes utterly deny the impending and inevitable death of a family member. These families no doubt are protecting themselves from what they fear will be the overwhelming pain of admitting the "unthinkable." Such fears in families deserve respect. When families are able to share their concerns and fears, however, they can touch and support one another at new levels of emotional depth that may enhance the quality of family relationships in the future.

Anger is a common emotion in chronic illness (Gilder et al., 1978). An ill person may be furious about what has happened and resentful that others are healthy while he or she is sick. This anger may be directed at healthy family members, at clinicians, at God, or it may be turned inward, blaming oneself for the illness. Family members may also be angry at the family member for getting sick, at the illness itself for bringing added burdens and responsibilities, and at God or fate for the threatened loss. This anger is often not expressed for fear of exacerbating the ill person's despair. Family members also feel guilty for being angry at someone who is ill and dependent (Wasow, 1985), and for being healthy and able to enjoy life in a way their loved one cannot (Gardner, 1969).

In most families with serious chronic illness, there is grief and depression. Families must grieve the loss of the healthy family member and the previous way of life of a family without illness. If the family cannot acknowledge and grieve these losses, chronic depression may result and lead to more difficulties in adapting to the illness. Many persons with serious chronic illness are depressed, and depression is a contagious emotion in families.

The psychiatrist Elizabeth Kübler-Ross (1969) and others have described stages that ill persons go through when facing death, including denial, anger, depression, and resolution. This model has been used to describe adaptations to chronic illness, although re-searchers have questioned the strict temporal sequencing suggested by Kübler-Ross. The ill individual and other family members often go through the same emotional responses. They are, however, frequently out of sync with one another (Baker, 1987). For example, because family members do not directly experience the pain and disability of an illness, they may be able to deny its existence or severity for a longer time than the ill person can. Although there are no systematic studies on this issue, it seems intuitively clear that it is more difficult for family members to share their feelings about an illness if they are at different stages in their emotional responses. A spouse who is struggling with anger and guilt may have difficulty listening to and acknowledging the ill person's grief or accept that person's calm resolve to die.

This section has described how families interact around the presence of chronic illness, particularly serious chronic illness. The onset of acute serious illness taxes the family's short-term emergency responses. But when an illness becomes chronic, the family must adjust to the presence of a new family "member"—the disease. Previous family patterns of inclusion, control, and intimacy must be revised to incorporate this new reality. As David Reiss (1981) has articulated, the family's paradigm or worldview—its image of itself as it relates to its environment—undergoes a transformation. In the model developed by the family researchers Hamilton McCubbin and Joan Patterson (1983), the family must struggle to achieve a level of adaptation to the chronic illness that allows for a balance between individual family members' needs and the family unit, and allows the family to relate positively with the outside world. That many families successfully handle these challenges, forging a new paradigm and successfully adapting to the illness, testifies to the rich resources of family strength, flexibility, and endurance.

The next section will focus the discussion more particularly around one of the most common and troublesome chronic illnesses—diabetes mellitus.

DIABETES AND THE FAMILY

Diabetes is a hereditary disease associated with a lack of insulin secretion by the pancreas, which prevents normal use of glucose or blood sugar for metabolism. In Type I diabetes, sometimes called juvenile-onset diabetes, the pancreas secretes no insulin, and the patient requires regular injections of insulin. In Type II diabetes, sometimes called adult-onset diabetes, the pancreas secretes insulin but in insufficient amounts; these patients' diabetes can frequently be controlled if they lose weight. According to the National Center for Health Statistics (1986), there are 5.8 million diabetics in the United States. Fully half of diabetics are limited in their daily activities, as compared to 15 per 1000 of the general population. Even with age controlled statistically, diabetics are twice as likely as the rest of the population to perceive themselves in fair or poor health (National Center for Health Statistics, 1986).

A large number of studies have demonstrated a relationship between family functioning and control of diabetes (Anderson & Auslander, 1980; Johnson, 1980; Klus et al., 1983). In a study of 20 preadolescent diabetics and their families, the pediatric nurse Margaret Grey and colleagues (1980) found that overall family dysfunction was strongly correlated with poor diabetic control. The Finnish researchers M. L. Koski and A. Kumento (1977) found a similar relationship between family functioning and diabetic control in a study of 60 diabetic children and their families. Most of the families of 30 poorly controlled diabetic children studied by the pediatrician Kimberly White and colleagues (1984) had numerous "dysfunctional" psychosocial factors, including absent fathers, poor living conditions, inadequate parental functioning, chronic family conflict, and lack of family involvement with the diabetes. Similar findings were obtained by pediatrician Donald Orr and his colleagues (1983) at the University of California, Irvine. On the other hand, clear order and organization in the family has been associated with good metabolic control (Shouval et al., 1982). High parental self-esteem is also associated with good control and has been found to be an important mediating factor between family functioning and diabetes (Grey et al., 1980).

Family cohesion seems to be particularly important in diabetes management. Both extremely low and extremely high cohesion have been associated with poor blood sugar control. In one of the earliest studies in this area, researchers A. Fischer and H. Dolger (1946) identified two common parental reactions to diabetes: overprotection and rejection. The overprotective parent had either a submissive or a rebellious adolescent diabetic, while the rejecting parent had a resentful and belligerent diabetic child. In a carefully controlled study, the diabetes researcher Barbara Anderson and colleagues (1981) found that low cohesion and high conflict were associated with poor diabetic control. Parental indifference can result in the worst diabetic control and lead to depression in the diabetic child (Khurana & White, 1970). In these disengaged families, poor diabetic control seems to result from lack of compliance with insulin and diet, due in part to inadequate supervision and support from parents.

Salvador Minuchin, Lester Baker, Bernice Rosman, and colleagues (1975, 1978) have described a group of poorly controlled diabetic children in families with excessively high cohesion. These children had recurrent episodes of diabetic ketoacidosis, despite adherence to diet and insulin. When hospitalized and removed from the family environment, their diabetes was easily managed. In these families and the families of children with severe asthma and anorexia nervosa, Minuchin discovered a specific pattern of interaction, which included enmeshment, overprotectiveness, rigidity, and conflict avoidance. In an experimental study (Baker et al., 1975), this research team studied the physiologic responses of three groups of diabetic children to a stressful family interview. Only the psychosomatic diabetics had a rise in free fatty acids (a precursor to the dangerous condition of diabetic ketoacidosis) during the family interview, an elevation that persisted after the interview. The parents of these children exhibited an initial rise in free fatty acid levels, which fell to normal when the child entered the room. The authors suggest that these diabetics are overinvolved or enmeshed in their parents' problems and respond to the stress with a rise in free fatty acids, which they cannot "turn off," resulting in diabetic ketoacidosis. In a larger sample of diabetic families, the Swedish psychiatrist Marianne Cederblad and colleagues (1982) were able to demonstrate that high family cohesion reported by the mother, family rigidity reported by the father, and anxiety in the diabetic child were all associated with poor metabolic control. Minuchin and colleagues (1975) have also reported the successful treatment of these diabetics and their psychosomatic families using structural family therapy to help disengage the diabetic and establish more appropriate family boundaries. In all 15 cases, the pattern of recurrent ketoacidosis ceased and insulin doses were reduced.

These studies suggest that the mechanisms by which the family influences diabetic control depend upon the style of family functioning, especially its cohesion. Both extremely high and extremely low cohesion are associated with poor diabetic control. In enmeshed families, diabetic control is physiologically linked to emotional processes within the family. In disengaged families, inadequate family structure and support results in noncompliance. These findings are consistent with the Circumplex Model of Family Functioning developed by the family researchers David Olson, Douglas Sprenkle, and Candace Russell (1979). They posit that midrange levels of cohesion and adaptability are associated with optimal family functioning in the face of stressful situations. While this model and the research findings on diabetes suggest specific clinical interventions for different types of families, no controlled studies have been conducted yet.

CASE ILLUSTRATION 2

Jim S. was a 16-year-old boy with poorly controlled diabetes mellitus. His diabetes was diagnosed at age 10 when he was hospitalized in a coma from diabetic ketoacidosis (DKA). Since that time, he has had eight hospital admissions for DKA and four for complications of his diabetes. He said that he complied with his diet, gave himself two injections of insulin a day, and checked his own blood sugars, yet his blood sugars remained very elevated. During that time, Jim began having problems at home and school. He flunked three of his courses and was suspended for possessing marijuana at school. He fought frequently with his stepfather, expressed affection only for his mother, and refused to do any household chores.

Jim's parents were quite concerned about his diabetes, but felt helpless. When they reminded him about his diet or insulin, he became furious and consumed an entire box of cookies. His parents frequently called his physician for help, and requested that he be hospitalized for an extended period of time to "really get his diabetes under control."

Jim's diabetes was only one of many problems with which this family was coping. Mr. and Mrs. S. recently had an unplanned pregnancy, followed closely by Mr. S. losing his job and then Mrs. S. developing a number of pregnancy- related medical problems. Soon after the baby was born, the family home burned to the ground. The family then moved three times over the next six months. The public health nurse sent out to check on the baby literally could not find the family.

This case illustrates a number of common family dynamics associated with adolescent insulin dependent diabetes, particularly problems of *inclusion* (Jim's alliance with one parent, the parents' desire to extrude Jim from the family by sending him to the hospital) and *control* (frequent conflict over his diabetes regimen and household responsibilities). We can safely assume that not much intimacy is possible under these circumstances. The case also shows the power of other life events influencing the family as it copes with a chronic illness. McCubbin and Patterson (1983) term this latter phenomenon the "pileup" of life events that can diminish the family's capacity to manage the strains connected with chronic illness. Chronic illness does not exist in a family vacuum. Life goes on for families, sometimes in ways that help them organize effectively around the chronic illness, and sometimes in ways that leave them struggling for survival.

INTERACTIONS OF HEALTH PROFESSIONALS AND FAMILIES WITH CHRONIC ILLNESS

Case Illustration 2 (continued)

Jim's poor control of his diabetes worried his physician as well as his parents. Dr. C. was in her last year of residency training in Family Medicine and had a small child of her own. At first, she became actively involved with the challenge of managing Jim's problems with diabetes. She tried to get Jim to take more control of his own illness by encouraging him to measure his blood sugars and adjust his insulin at home. She discouraged his parents' supervision of his diabetes, asking them to "treat him as an adult." Unfortunately, he frequently missed his appointments and would arrive in the emergency room in mild diabetic ketoacidosis. The emergency room physicians would suggest to Dr. C. that she should get his blood sugars under better control, so that he wouldn't end up in the hospital.

Dr. C. alternated between being understanding with Jim, feeling the parents were to blame because they were so intrusive, and being very angry with the boy for not taking care of himself. She would lecture him on the importance of diabetic control and how he might lose his legs, go blind, or die if he didn't take better care of himself. Like the parents, she felt helpless and unable to control Jim's diabetes, and resorted to hospitalization as a way to relieve the pressure in the therapeutic triangle and gain some control. She was relieved when she finished her training and was able to pass his care on to an incoming resident in her program.

In this section, we add the health care system to our analysis of families with chronic illness. The interactions between health professionals and families can mirror those occurring within families. As the family researcher Lisa Baker and the family physician Michael Pontious have maintained, conceptual models useful for understanding family dynamics can be extended to other systems, including the health care "family" (Baker & Pontious, 1984). We will again use the Family FIRO model to organize issues concerning the interactions of health professionals with families experiencing chronic illness.

**Inclusion Issues Between
Health Professionals and Families**

In caring for families with chronic illness, clinicians must decide how involved to be. This level of involvement can range from being detached or disengaged from the family, often by referring them to a specialist for all their care, to being intimately connected or enmeshed with the family. Some clinicians are fearful of getting involved with a family and choose to remain disconnected. Some families do not allow the clinician to become close. Such distant clinical relationships rarely allow health professionals to help the family with the psychosocial face of chronic illness.

On the other hand, some clinicians wish to save families suffering with chronic illness, and may become a quasi-family member. The clinician overreacts emotionally to each problem and each crisis the family faces, and thus is unable to maintain the outsider's perspective necessary to help the family. Most clinicians believe that the therapeutic ideal involves a collaborative working relationship with the family, in which the clinician remains in a balanced position: well connected with the family without becoming engulfed in the family's experience.

As described in preceding chapters, Doherty and Baird (1983) have conceptualized clinician/patient/family relationships as a "therapeutic triangle" in which each party influences the relationship between the other two. They warn of the dangers of treating the patient in isolation or joining with just the patient against the family or with the family against the patient. The family therapist Peggy Penn (1983) has described these coalitions between clinicians and family members. Clinicians who do not have a family systems perspective on health care may try to exclude the family from the patient's care by not inviting them to appointments, or by not seeking or acknowledging their opinions. Such a coalition between the provider and the patient against the family may lead to conflict between the family and the clinician, which frequently is detrimental to caring for the illness. This interaction seems to occur most commonly when both the family and the health professional are in a centripetal phase of development. The young clinician, struggling with autonomy issues, overidentifies with the adolescent and joins with the adolescent against the rest of the family.

Control Issues Between
Health Professionals and Families

Health professionals in mainstream North American culture, and physicians in particular, are most comfortable when they feel in control of the treatment process and are uneasy when not in control. The dominant cultural image in medicine is the physician in charge of the acute life-threatening illness in the intensive care unit of the hospital. The physician controls everything that happens to the patient: what kind of treatment the patient receives, which medicines, when they are administered, and so on. When this approach is applied to patients with chronic illness, it leads to major conflicts around control. For example, if clinicians feel responsible for how high a diabetic's blood sugar is, they are likely to first encourage and then try to coerce patients into better compliance with diet and insulin. If patients feel their autonomy is threatened, they may resist and be noncompliant in order to maintain personal control over the illness. As mentioned in previous chapters, Ross and Phipps (1986, p. 100) have argued that, for some patients, noncompliance helps to maintain a balance of power between patient and provider: "Paradoxically, in order to be in control, the patient [has] to be out of control vis-à-vis the medical problem." Thus the harder the provider attempts to exert control, the less the positive influence on the patient. As one patient with severe emphysema explained, "Doctor, when you get after me about my smoking, I get nervous and smoke even more." This conflict over control is usually covert. The patient agrees verbally that compliance is a good idea, but claims to be helpless, or passively remains "unable" to make the recommended changes.

When family members are in a struggle with the patient over control and responsibility for the illness, they may try to enlist the clinician's support for their view of the problem. Family members may call the clinician to report on patient's noncompliance and offer to serve as a "spy" for the clinician. A coalition between the family and health professional is likely to result in power struggles between the clinician and patient, and to increasing problems with noncompliance. What is most productive and healing is a collaborative, noncontrolling alliance of the health professional with both the patient and the family.

Intimacy Issues Between
Health Professionals and Families

It is at this phase of the Family Health and Illness Cycle that intimacy between clinicians and families is most common. It may also occur in the care of healthy families over many years, through sharing the trials of normal growth and development and acute medical problems. The intense emotional experience of chronic illness for clinicians and families, however, promotes close personal relationships. The sheer endurance of these relationships over many years creates the possibility of trust and self-disclosure. For intimacy to develop, families must be willing to share their emotions, and clinicians must be willing to hear and accept these emotions. Families may not want to reveal their negative experiences with the illness, because they fear appearing weak, because they desire to reassure the clinician (and themselves) that they are a "good" family, or because they hold a magical belief that if the powerful clinician thinks all is going well, then all must be going well (Sabbeth, 1984).

Clinicians care for many suffering people and must protect themselves from being overwhelmed by the pain and grief of their patients. To be intimate is to feel some of the suffering and helplessness of these families and, at appropriate times, to share with the family one's personal feelings and experiences. Helpless feelings are particularly difficult for clinicians to experience and share. As the psychologist Barbara Sabbeth (1984) has stated, "It is difficult to empathize with another person in distress, when there is little you can do to change the circumstances causing the problems." Clinicians who accept their personal and professional limits, however, and who are able to share their feelings with their own family, friends, and trusted professional colleagues, are better able to tolerate the risks of being intimate with patients and families whose problems cannot be resolved by any clinician, no matter how skillful.

Case Illustration 1 (continued)

> When Jill was first diagnosed as having rheumatoid arthritis, her family physician, Dr. N., met with her and her husband Steve in their home. He discussed the results of her tests and implications of the diagnosis. He answered some of their questions and offered to find the answers to others. He encouraged them to share their fears and frustrations, while resisting his own desire to reassure them that all would be well. They discussed what role he would play in Jill's care, and Dr. N. agreed to help coordinate and supervise her care among the numerous specialists, and be available to answer questions and discuss concerns. He referred them to the local chapter of the Arthritis Foundation.
>
> Over the course of Jill's illness, Dr. N. has become quite close to Jill and Steve, and has helped them through several major crises. He shared with them his own sense of frustration and helplessness in preventing the progression of the illness and Jill's disability. They have shared with him the pain and suffering their family has endured, and their fears of what the future will bring.

IMPLICATIONS FOR HEALTH PROFESSIONALS WORKING WITH FAMILIES WITH CHRONIC ILLNESS

The most basic need of families with chronic illness is factual information about the disease. Health professionals should educate patients and their families about the etiology, treatment, and prognosis of the illness, and be available to answer questions. Families want access to reasonable expectations for what the ill person can do and what the family should provide. Some families need specific advice about how to cope with the illness, or help with solving illness-related problems. Once their needs for information and practical advice are met, many families are open to discussing their feelings and fears related to the illness and its effects on their lives.

To work effectively with these families, the clinician must join with the patient and family and obtain their trust. This is best done by meeting with the entire family at the time of the diagnosis in order to explain the illness, discuss their concerns, and answer questions. Periodic follow-up meetings with the patient and family will help to avoid misunderstandings and coalitions. When the mother is defined by the family as the principle caretaker of a chronically ill child, it is especially important to invite the father to family conferences and to encourage him to participate actively in his child's care. When a chronic illness enters a stable phase, or develops into the terminal phase, there is a strong pull for health professionals to withdraw from the patient and family out of self-protection and because they feel "there is nothing more to offer." This is usually when the family needs the clinician's personal involvement and support the most.

When patients are referred to specialists for care, the primary care clinician should remain in contact with both the family and all the members of the health care team, especially consultants. This clinician is responsible for assuring that the care is coordinated with clearly delineated roles for the different professionals involved. Keeping in contact with all members of the team will help to avoid conflicts and coalitions within the treatment system. While this clinician is usually the primary care physician or nurse practitioner, other health professionals, including social workers and family therapists, can assist in the coordination of care. In addition, they can help families develop appropriate collaborative relationships with their physicians and teach them to communicate effectively and assertively with the health care professionals.

When families experience problems involving closeness or inclusion, the clinician can assist in establishing more appropriate and adaptive boundaries within the family. For disengaged families, this may involve inviting the family to each medical appointment and asking for their help in the care of the patient. In some cases, simply educating the family about the illness and how they can assist will help them become more involved. With enmeshed families, the clinician needs to draw boundaries around the patient as the one who has the illness, while simultaneously remaining in a collaborative mode with the family.

During appointments, the clinician can first meet alone with the patient and then with the family. Rigidly enmeshed families often need referral to a family therapist for assistance.

Health professionals are well advised to avoid power struggles with patients or families over control of the chronic illness. The clinician must recognize that patients are ultimately responsible for their own health care, and that clinicians can only assist patients and their families to assume that care. The clinician can negotiate with the family the roles and responsibilities that the clinician will have in the care of the illness. For example, a public health nurse may need to negotiate with a diabetic patient and the family about who will prepare the insulin syringes, give the injections, monitor the blood sugars, and supervise the diet. This approach not only encourages self-care but can serve as a model for helping the family negotiate their other responsibilities.

Such open negotiation, however, sometimes will lead to agreements that might not be popular with the clinician's colleagues, as in the case of an obese diabetic woman who was tired of trying to lose weight. She and her physician agreed that she would accept her current weight, knowing that her blood sugar levels would be higher than desirable, and that her physician who do his best medically within the limits that her obesity imposed on diabetes control. Her family members also agreed to stop nagging her about her weight. This agreement preserved a collaborative physician/patient/family relationship and allowed for the possibility of constructive change in the future if the patient decided to modify her life-style priorities.

The clinician can facilitate family intimacy by providing a safe and supportive environment for families to share their feelings about the illness. In the presence of the clinician, anger, guilt, and sadness can be expressed and validated. Normalizing statements such as the following are one effective way of eliciting unexpressed emotions: "Many family members feel a great deal of frustration and anger toward the illness, the health professionals, and even the person who is sick." When anger is directed toward members of the health care team, the clinician must honestly assess the family's concerns and avoid becoming defensive. If mistakes have been made, they should be acknowledged and a corrective plan established. Very often, anger about the illness is directed toward health professionals because they cannot do more, and this should also be acknowledged: "I understand how angry you are that we cannot do more to help. I too wish there was more we could do!"

Allowing a family to share their grief and sadness with each other and with the clinician can be a powerful and therapeutic experience. Well-meaning friends of the family usually try to encourage them, emphasizing any improvements or hopes. The family may begin to believe that they shouldn't feel discouraged, but rather grateful because things could be worse. It is a tremendous relief for the family to hear a trusted professional acknowledge and understand their suffering as well as their hope.

Individual clinicians cannot provide all the services and support that families with chronic illness need. A collaborative health team should include physicians, nurses, social workers, psychologists, physical therapists, family therapists, nutritionists, and others in order to offer a wide range of services needed by these families. In addition, clinicians should familiarize themselves with multifamily groups and self-help organizations oriented toward specific illnesses. These organizations can provide education and emotional support and help with coping skills and advocacy (see Lubkin, 1986, for names and addresses of many of these organizations).

CONCLUSION

The Chinese character for crisis consists of two symbols that stand for danger and opportunity. Many chronic illnesses bring a crisis that severely stresses families and threatens to disrupt them. It can also be an opportunity to change old dysfunctional patterns to develop new, healthier patterns of inclusion, control, and intimacy through the shared experiences of coping with illness.

Some chronic illnesses such as hypertension are relatively silent members of families. Although their consequences may come suddenly and sometimes fatally, their daily presence, except for efforts to comply with medication and diet, is generally not seriously stressful for families. At the other extreme are progressive, degenerative chronic illnesses that impair an individual's daily functioning. These individuals must reorder their personal priorities, adapt to their physical limitations, and create a new self-image. Their families must grieve the loss of their family member's health and accept a restructuring of the family. Their clinicians must shift from curing illness to caring for illness, and work collaboratively with patients and families to help them cope and reach their highest potential. Serious chronic illness presents a litmus test for the humanity of us all.

DISCUSSION QUESTIONS

(1) Consider a chronic illness that has affected someone in your nuclear family or extended family. How has your family adapted itself to the illness? How do you think your family has influenced the course of the illness?

(2) What is the relationship between family functioning and the control of diabetes? What is the role of noncompliance in poor diabetic control?

(3) How can the interactions between patient and health professional reflect patterns of interactions within the patient's family? How can clinicians avoid becoming caught up in negative family interaction patterns?

RECOMMENDED READINGS

Crouch, M., & Roberts, L. (Eds.). (1987). *The family in medical practice: A family systems primer*. New York: Springer-Verlag.

Lubkin, I. M. (1986). *Chronic illness: Impact and intervention*. Boston: Jones and Bartlett.

Minuchin, S., Rosman, B. L., & Baker, L. (1978). *Psychosomatic families*. Cambridge, MA: Harvard University Press.

National Institute of Mental Health. (1986). *Family's Impact on Health: A Critical Review and Annotated Bibliography* (T. L. Campbell, Author). Series DN, No. 6; DHHS Pub. No. (ADM) 86-1461. Washington, DC: Superintendent of Documents, Government Printing Office.

CHAPTER

7

Summary and Implications

PREVIOUS CHAPTERS HAVE FOLLOWED the sequence of the Family Health and Illness Cycle by describing how families deal with a variety of illnesses. This chapter summarizes the cycle by taking one disease—coronary heart disease—through its course with the family. In addition, we also present research and clinical issues facing the field of family and health in the late 1980s.

CORONARY HEART
DISEASE IN THE FAMILY
HEALTH AND ILLNESS CYCLE

Coronary heart disease (CHD) appears to be attracting more positive health promotion and risk reduction efforts by individuals and families than any other disease. These efforts are supported by a consensus among health professionals that cigarette smoking and high cholesterol levels in the blood cause heart disease. A wide range of evidence cited in this volume attests to the importance of family relationships in individuals' smoking and eating behaviors. While progress in these areas has been impressive, resulting in a decrease in death from heart disease, large numbers of individuals and families continue to engage in health behaviors, smoking in particular, that are injurious to their health (Center for Disease Control, 1986).

Preventing heart disease often leads to troublesome interactions among family members and among patients, families, and health care professionals. Individuals engaging in high-risk behaviors are sensitive to the difference between "encouraging" and "nagging" from family members (Doherty et al., 1983). High-risk patients who continue to smoke cigarettes are a source of frustration for many clinicians and a source of concern for many family members. The result often is a series of control struggles over the risky behavior, with the patient becoming more stubborn as the clinician and family become more persistent.

For coronary heart disease, the Vulnerability and Disease Onset/Relapse phase of the cycle represents the time when symptoms of the disease manifest themselves, usually in angina (chest pain) or in acute myocardial infarction (heart attack). Here the individual, family, and clinician are dealing with the emergence of a life-threatening situation. Although the family factors in CHD at this stage have not been investigated extensively, an indirect link seems clear in the literature linking psychosocial stress and support with the onset of angina and myocardial infarction. The family physician Jack Medalie and his colleague U. Goldbourt (1976) found that Israeli men who rated themselves most happily married were least likely to experience the onset of angina over a five-year period. Other studies have found that psychosocial stress is associated with increased risk for a fatal recurrent heart attack (Ruberman et al., 1984). Cardiologists such as Richard Kones (1979) hypothesize that stress enhances the activity of catecholamine hormones in the blood, which in turn affects the heart's blood vessels and electrophysiologic condition. The same processes have been suggested for the link between Type A behavior pattern (hard driving, competitive, angry) and the onset of CHD (Williams et al., 1982).

Family Illness Appraisal in CHD concerns the ways that families construe the symptoms being experienced by the family member, their decision about seeking medical treatment, and their ideas about the causes, consequences, and course of CHD once it is diagnosed (Leventhal et al., 1985). Of particular interest in myocardial infarction is the tendency of individuals and families to minimize the seriousness of the symptoms and delay seeking help. Because the idea of a heart attack is terribly frightening, the victim and the family may conspire to ignore the significance of classic symptoms such as chest pain. A common example is a man with chest pain climbing a flight of stairs in order to "prove" that he is not having a heart attack. On the other extreme from denial are families with an angina patient who assume that every chest pain means the onset of a fatal heart attack. Once treatment has been initiated, family illness appraisal will be influenced by the willingness of clinicians to share information and offer emotional support for the family. Unclear or indirect communication between clinicians and patients and families can lead to persistent misdefinitions of the illness.

Example: A consulting cardiologist told a patient that he had had a heart attack, but the primary care physician, assuming that the cardiologist had made everything clear, never confirmed that diagnosis in conversations with the patient. The patient and his wife decided to "agree" with their own doctor that the chest pain episode was something other than a heart attack—probably indigestion (the chest pain) and arthritis (the pain radiating to the left arm). A breakdown in communication with clinicians contributed to a distorted family illness appraisal that led the patient to take no preventive measures to avoid a recurrent myocardial infarction.

Family Acute Response to CHD is best represented in the crisis precipitated by a heart attack. As the psychologist Howard Leventhal and his colleagues (1985, p. 125) have stated, "With death looming, all [family] efforts are focused on its avoidance: The goal is the preservation of life." Unlike the case of cancer, there generally are few decisions for the family to make once medical treatment has begun. When clinician/family communication is clear and supportive, the family is apt to rally its resources to cope with the emergency. There may be some recriminations (such as asking an adolescent son why he let his father shovel the sidewalk and bring on a heart attack), but generally the family pulls together over the short haul to see the patient and one another through the crisis. Based on his study of 20 families in which the husband had experienced a sudden onset heart attack, the family therapist Ross Carter (1984, p. 57) gives the following description of the families' acute response:

> The families . . . immediately developed an emergency reaction pattern characterized by constriction of activity, mobilization of resources, readiness for action, and a centralization of focus. Ordinary activity was suspended as the family attended to, and organized around, the threat of potential loss of a central leading person. . . . Even though the nuclear family tightly coalesced, extended kin were activated and boundaries around the nuclear family were suspended, as representatives from the kinship network joined to provide structural and psychological support

by fulfilling roles temporarily abandoned by nuclear family members. . . .
Uncertainty of outcome created a condition of readiness for action rather
than activity. It is as if the family was geared for battle but was uncertain
as to whether war would be declared. This condition created a high
degree of dependency on physicians, nursing staff, and the hospital.

The Family Adaptation phase in CHD begins when the acute
emergency is over, in the case of myocardial infarction, or when the
disease has assumed a presumably permanent role in the family's life. A
unique stress of CHD is the possibility of sudden death; most other
diseases take their toll over time. A second major stress of CHD stems
from patients and families' efforts to come to terms with life-style factors
such as diet and smoking that directly affect the likelihood of a
recurrent heart attack. A third significant issue is the extent to which
the heart attack patient can return to previous roles; Carter's (1984)
clinical study particularly noted the importance of whether the husband
returns to his work role. These stresses force families to confront
powerful inclusion, control, and intimacy issues during the adaptation
phase. Inclusion issues concern fear of losing the family member,
withdrawal from active shared family activities, the prospect of early
retirement with consequences for the couple's companionship time,
role renegotiation, and threats to the patient's autonomy. Control
issues include power struggles over medication taking, smoking, and
diet, and conflict over changing roles and life-styles. Intimacy issues
include returning to sexual closeness for the couple, and the willingness
to share feelings and fears related to the heart disease and the
possibility of sudden death.

The Family Adaptation phase is also the most trying for clinicians. In
the acute phase of CHD, the family generally concedes control to
clinicians, who by training are predisposed to assume complete control
over the patient's care. During the chronic phase, the patient and family
take back some of this control—whether through cooperation with the
clinicians or through noncooperation. As opposed to the intense
connection during hospitalization, the family's association with their
clinicians in the adjustment phase is likely to oscillate between distance
and closeness, with little contact for many months, followed by closer
contact when further tests or procedures are required, and then
intense contact when a relapse occurs. These issues are further
complicated by the nature of the therapeutic triangle: The clinician may
be connected with the patient but cut off from the family, or joined with
the family but in a coalition that distances the patient.

This discussion illustrates the dynamic nature of families' experience with illness as described in the Family Health and Illness Cycle. As the family reaches resolution or stability in one phase, it concentrates on the next. Some of the family's coping efforts in the adaptation phase of CHD, for example, may be extended and redefined as efforts at health promotion and risk reduction. In other words, when the heart attack is well in the past, the threat of sudden death feels remote, and roles have been successfully renegotiated, the family may be viewed less as still "adjusting" and more as enhancing health in order to prevent a relapse. With CHD, some families go through the cycle several times when heart attacks recur.

The Family Health and Illness Cycle also represents the phases of the clinician's experience with the illness, the patient, and the family. The most stressful time during the cycle for the family may also be the most difficult for the clinician. Particularly during the vulnerability/on-set and illness-appraisal phases of symptoms that lack a clear diagnosis, the anxiety levels of families and clinicians alike are apt to be high. When families panic, they put enormous pressure on clinicians (particularly physicians) to take decisive action, often to hospitalize or perform sometimes unnecessary, dangerous, and costly tests. Clinicians have their own anxieties and fears of making a mistake and of disappointing the patient and family. As our colleague Macaran Baird frequently points out in clinical situations, it is sometimes difficult to decide what we are primarily treating: our own anxiety, the patient's or family's anxiety, or the disease process (all of which, of course, are interconnected). Treating anxiety in the guise of biological disease is a costly process in human and economic terms. The alternative, as Doherty and Baird (1987) point out in their discussion of family-centered medical care, is for clinicians to summon the courage to deal directly with their own anxiety and that of the families whose lives they encounter at frightening moments.

RESEARCH ON
FAMILIES AND HEALTH

In 1979, Theodur Litman and Maureen Venters, from the School of Public Health at the University of Minnesota, wrote: "Despite increased interest on the part of behavioral scientists in the role of the family in health and illness, empirical research has remained relatively limited, plagued by methodological imprecision and minimal integration with family theory" (Litman & Venters, 1979). While there has been a substantial growth in family and health research during the 1980s, many of the same theoretical and methodological problems persist.

Theoretical Models in Family and Health Research

Much of the existing research on families and health lacks theory. That is, the relationships between family variables and aspects of health and illness are empirically linked without clear ideas for how they might influence each other. The result is stray findings without benefit of an explanatory model. Theory helps the investigator to decide what questions to ask, what variables to measure, and how to analyze and interpret the data. We will briefly review several theoretical models that have proved useful in family and health research.

Stress theory considers life events or conditions as potential stressors that make demands upon individuals and families and may result in maladaptation, dysfunction, or illness (Pearlin et al., 1981). Studies on the impact of illness on families have considered illness to be a stressor that can cause psychological problems in other family members. For example, there is a large body of literature on the effect of childhood illnesses on siblings and mothers (see Chapter 6 in this volume). *Family stress theory* was developed by the family sociologist Reuben Hill (1949, 1958) in his ABCX model. This framework considers how the family as a whole adapts to stressful situations, depending upon its perception of the event and its resources for dealing with the situation. Family stress theory has been developed further by Hamilton McCubbin and Joan Patterson (1983) and used to study families' responses to chronic illnesses. In their *Double ABCX model of Family Adaptation*, McCubbin and Patterson focus on several factors relevant to chronic illness that were not considered in Hill's original model, specifically, the "pileup" of stressful life events in families dealing with chronic illness, the family's new resources mobilized after the onset of the illness, the family's ongoing perceptions of their situation, its ongoing coping activities, and its resulting level of adaptation to a chronic illness. McCubbin and Patterson have developed a series of instruments to measure the concepts in their model, which has assumed an important place in research on families and health.

In medicine, *social epidemiology* is the predominant theoretical framework for explaining the influence of psychosocial factors on health. Derived from the infectious disease model, this theory views psychosocial stressors as lowering the individual's resistance to disease agents, and views social support as either buffering the effects of stress or independently improving the resistance to illness (Cassel, 1976). In this model, the family may be a source of stress (e.g., bereavement, divorce, stressful family events) or social support (e.g., marriage, support by children). Because this research is based in epidemiology, it is very quantitative and tends to measure very simple family measures (e.g., marital status, death of a spouse) in large populations.

Both family stress theory and social epidemiology tend to be linear or unidirectional, that is, they consider either the effects of illness on the family or vice versa. General systems theory, developed by the biologist Ludwig von Bertalanffy (1968) and others in response to the narrowness of traditional scientific methods, was extended to clinical medicine by Engel (1977) in the *biopsychosocial model*. Systems theory and the biopsychosocial model assume that there are complex and multi-directional interactions between biological, psychological, and social processes. Because of the complexities of these interactions, research based on systems theory tends to be more descriptive and qualitative than other research in the family and health field (Doherty, Baird, & Becker, 1987).

Family systems theory, an organizing framework for this volume, has been applied extensively to family and health issues in the 1980s, but its contributions have been more in the clinical domain than in research. An exception is David Reiss's (1981) Family Paradigms model, which has emerged as a promising framework for understanding how families organize themselves around chronic and life-threatening illness. The Family FIRO model, described in Chapter 6, is a recent attempt to create a family systems model of family and health that lends itself to qualitative and quantitative research.

In summary, there are several useful theoretical models that researchers can use to guide their investigations and organize their findings. The field of families and health, as reflected in the phases of the Family Health and Illness Cycle, is too large and complex to be reduced to a generally accepted theory in the foreseeable future. In the meantime, current theories can serve as important guideposts as we develop better models with further study.

Research Designs in
Families and Health

The vast majority of studies on families and health have been cross-sectional in design, that is, they measure variables at one point in time. This is the easiest and least expensive way to examine associations between family factors and health. Large numbers of subjects can be studied, thus increasing the generalizability of the study. These investigations have been particularly useful for examining whether certain types of family structure, communication, or interactions are associated with certain illnesses (diabetes, asthma, and anorexia nervosa). A frequent problem in these studies, however, is the interpretation of their results. Correlations may be due to the family affecting the illness, the illness affecting the family, or because of other important factors such as genetics, medication effects, or the treatment context. In the cloud of correlated processes that make up families' experiences with health and illness, it is difficult to tease out which processes take priority in influencing others.

Problems associated with cross-sectional designs can be alleviated somewhat by the use of well-selected control groups. To determine whether family variables are specific for certain illnesses, control families should include not only normal (non-ill) families, but families with other acute or chronic illnesses. For example, cross-sectional studies by psychiatrists Lyman Wynne and Margaret Singer (1963a, 1963b; Singer & Wynne, 1965) established that parents of schizophrenics had deviant styles of communication that were not observed in normal families or families with other psychopathology.

Prospective cohort studies, in which the researchers begin to study families prior to the onset of an illness, are expensive and difficult to conduct, but allow one to determine whether family factors precede and potentially affect an illness. Studies that attempt to determine the role of the family in the onset or etiology of an illness need either very large samples (e.g., the Israeli Ischemic Heart Study—Medalie & Goldbourt, 1976), or samples of subjects at high risk for a disorder (e.g., the UCLA Family Study of Schizophrenia—Doane et al., 1985). Prospective studies of the course or treatment of an already existing illness are much easier to conduct and have been underutilized by investigators. Many social support studies use a variant of this prospective design, called a retrospective cohort study, in which data have been collected prospectively for another study and are reexamined later by a researcher. Such a technique allowed the family researcher Jeri Doane and colleagues (1981) to assess the affective style of families with disturbed adolescents from videotapes that had been made at the start of the prospective study for another purpose.

To determine adequately whether a family intervention or family therapy is effective, a randomized control trial (RCT) is necessary. Case studies in which the subjects "act as their own controls" are subject to numerous biases. Unfortunately, RCTs are the most difficult type of study to conduct. Donald Morisky and colleagues' (1983) trial of family involvement in hypertension compliance is an excellent model and offered persuasive evidence for the importance of the family in physical health. An additional problem in studying family therapy is the need for an appropriate comparison therapy. The best RCTs of family therapy are psychiatrist Ian Falloon and colleagues' (1982) study of schizophrenia, and psychologist M. Duncan Stanton and colleague T. C. Todd's (1982) work on heroin addiction.

Finally, family and health research has much to gain from qualitative methods that offer in-depth insight into a smaller number of cases. Termed "naturalistic inquiry" by the family physician Anton Kuzel (1986), this approach is exemplified by the work of the anthropologist Joan Ablon (1985) on family dynamics and alcoholism, and the work of the family physician Lucy Candib and her colleagues (1987) on the effect of a physician's pregnancy and childbearing on relationships with patients. Candib also has provided leadership in an emerging feminist critique of how women and families are studied and treated in contemporary medicine. Indeed, as discussed in Chapter 4, much of the family and health research literature assumes that the wife/mother will be the primary caretaker of sick family members. The next decade is apt to see a reevaluation of researchers' assumptions about male and female roles in the American family.

Family Measurement

A major methodological problem in family and health research is the paucity of reliable and valid methods of measuring families. Many studies have used unstructured, impressionistic assessments of the families or have developed elaborate assessment devices that lack standardization and tests of reliability and validity. Some of the better assessment tools consider only the marital subsystem (e.g., Marital Adjustment Scale—Locke & Wallace, 1959), or one dimension of family life such as parental communication (e.g., Family Rorschach—Singer & Wynne, 1965a), or expressed emotion (e.g., Camberwell Family Interview—Vaughn & Leff, 1976). Over the past decade, numerous instruments have been developed that attempt to measure the functioning of the entire family, and they are beginning to be used in studies on the family and health. Most of these rely exclusively on self-report by family members, and only a few use direct observations of families.

Forman and Hagan (1983) have reviewed the psychometric characteristics of six instruments designed to assess overall family functioning. These instruments included the Family Adaptability and Cohesion Evaluation Scale (FACES) (Olson, 1986; Olson et al., 1985), Family Environmental Scale (FES) (Moos, 1974), Family Functioning Index (Pless & Satterwhite, 1973), Family Concept Assessment Method (van der Veen, 1965), Family Assessment Device (Epstein et al., 1978) and the Beavers-Timberlawn Family Evaluation Scale (BTFES) (Lewis et al., 1976). A prominent measurement of family paradigms in interacting with the environment is Reiss's (1981) Card Sort Procedure. Most of these instruments appear to have reasonably good stability (test-retest reliability) and internal consistency, but less attention has been paid to validity, that is, the extent to which they measure what they are trying to measure. The few attempts to cross-validate different instruments (Oliveri & Reiss, 1984) have found no correlations between the instruments, even when they appeared to be measuring the same family attribute. It is not known whether this lack of agreement is a result of the different methods used (self-report versus observation), the concepts being measured, or the tests themselves.

Instruments for measuring family functioning are still at a primitive stage. Of those reviewed, it is not possible to determine which ones are universally better or more useful for research, although the FACES instrument, the Family Assessment Device, and the Card Sort Procedure are showing promise in the family and health area. Much more work on comparing these instruments is needed, both conceptually to clarify what aspects of the family they are attempting to measure, and methodologically to cross-validate them.

Overall, there has been insufficient attention paid to methodology in research on the family and health. Too many authors have inferred causal relationships from correlations found in cross-sectional studies. Nonstandardized family assessment techniques and unvalidated self-reports of illness are used too frequently. The strength of the evidence that shows that the family factors are strongly linked with health and illness is dependent on the quality of the methods used to study this relationship.

Despite these ongoing concerns about research on families and health, we are encouraged by interdisciplinary developments in the 1980s that are combining qualitative and quantitative methods, that measure biological as well as family dimensions, and that employ sophisticated statistical techniques. Funding for complex studies in families and health has been difficult to find, but there are winds of change in the federal government in the late 1980s, symbolized by formation in 1986 of the Health and Behavior Branch in the National Institute of Mental Health, which is explicitly committed to funding biopsychosocial research projects. If interdisciplinary cooperation continues to develop and federal funding opens up, the next decade of research on families and health promises to be the most exciting period in the field's history.

FAMILY INTERVENTIONS IN HEALTH CARE

Along with renewed interest in research, the family and health field has seen an upsurge in writing about clinical work with families dealing with health and illness issues. This development has been prominent both in family medicine and in nursing, as these two fields have reached out to family therapy. As clinicians began to experiment with family-centered health care, an important professional issue emerged immediately: What are appropriate family interventions for physicians and nurses to engage in without turning these primary care health professionals into would-be family therapists?

Leaders in both family medicine and family nursing responded in similar ways to this challenge of clarifying their role with families as distinct from the role of family therapists. New terms were created, such as "working with families," "primary care family counseling," and "family nursing"—each term used in contrast to family therapy. The goal has been to create a language that would allow the distinctive functions of primary care clinicians to be delineated without implying that these professionals can, without specialized training, serve in the same capacity as family therapists (Doherty, 1986). More recently, Doherty and Baird (1986, 1987) have proposed a five-level model of clinicians's involvement with families in health care contexts. This model, summarized in Table 7.1, breaks the primary care role into four

TABLE 7.1
Levels of Clinician Involvement with Families

Level 1: Minimal Emphasis on Family

This baseline level of involvement consists of dealing with families only as necessary for practical and medical/legal reasons, but not viewing communicating with families as integral to the clinician's role or as involving skills for the clinician to develop. This level presumably characterizes most medical school training where biomedical issues are the sole conscious focus of patient care.

Level 2: Ongoing Medical Information and Advice

Knowledge base: Primarily medical, plus awareness of the triangular dimension of the clinician-patient relationship.

Personal development: Openness to engage patients and families in a collaborative way.

Skills:

1. Regularly and clearly communicating medical findings and treatment options to family members.
2. Asking family members questions that elicit relevant diagnostic and treatment information.
3. Attentively listening to family members' questions and concerns.
4. Advising families about how to handle the medical and rehabilitation needs of the patient.
5. For large or demanding families, knowing how to channel communication through one or two key members.
6. Identifying gross family dysfunction that interferes with medical treatment, and referring the family to a therapist.

Level 4: Systematic Assessment and Planned Intervention

Knowledge base: Family Systems.

Personal development: Awareness of one's own participation in systems including the therapeutic triangle, the medical system, one's own family system, and larger community systems.

Skills:

1. Engaging family members, including reluctant ones, in a planned family conference or a series of conferences.
2. Structuring a conference with even a poorly communicating family in such a way that all members have a chance to express themselves.
3. Systematically assessing the family's level of functioning.
4. Supporting individual members while avoiding coalitions.
5. Reframing the family's definition of their problem in a way that makes problem solving more achievable.
6. Helping the family members view their difficulty as requiring new forms of collaborative efforts.
7. Helping the family members generate alternative, mutually acceptable ways to cope with their difficulty.
8. Helping the family balance their coping efforts by calibrating their various roles in a way that allows support without sacrificing anyone's autonomy.
9. Identifying family dysfunction that lies beyond primary care treatment and orchestrating a referral by educating the family and the therapist about what to expect from one another.

Level 3: Feelings and Support

Knowledge base: Normal family development and reactions to stress.

Personal development: Awareness of one's own feelings in relationship to the patient and family.

Skills:

1. Asking questions that elicit family members' expressions of concerns and feelings related to the patient's condition and its effect on the family.
2. Empathically listening to family members' concerns and feelings, and normalizing them where appropriate.
3. Forming a preliminary assessment of the family's level of functioning as it relates to the patient's problem.
4. Encouraging family members in their efforts to cope as a family with their situation.
5. Tailoring medical advice to the unique needs, concerns, and feelings of the family.
6. Identifying family dysfunction and fitting a referral recommendation to the unique situation of the family.

Level 5: Family Therapy

Knowledge base: Family Systems and patterns whereby dysfunctional families interact with professionals and other health care systems.

Personal development: Ability to handle intense emotions in families and self and to maintain neutrality in the face of strong pressure from family members or other professionals.

Skills:

The following is not an exhaustive list of family therapy skills but rather a list of several key skills that distinguish Level 5 involvement from primary care involvement with families.

1. Interviewing families or family members who are quite difficult to engage.
2. Efficiently generating and testing hypotheses about the family's difficulties and interaction patterns.
3. Escalating conflict in the family in order to break a family impasse.
4. Temporarily siding with one family member against another.
5. Constructively dealing with a family's strong resistance to change.
6. Negotiating collaborative relationships with other professionals and other systems who are working with the family, even when these groups are at odds with one another.

levels of increasing intensity, and adds a fifth level termed "family therapy." We will use this model to characterize the wide range of appropriate encounters between clinicians and families in health care. As summarized in Table 7.1, the model suggests the knowledge base, personal development base, and skills required of the clinician at each level of involvement. It was developed originally with physicians in mind; however, we believe the model is general enough to describe interactions between families and a wide variety of clinicians.

Level 1, *Minimal Emphasis on Family*, represents the level of involvement with families generally practiced by physicians at university hospitals and other tertiary care medical centers where medical students and residents are trained. The family is not regarded as a conscious object of attention and concern for clinicians, except insofar as practical and legal reasons require contact with the family. The individual patient is the sole focus of attention, and often the focus is only on the patient's disease process.

Level 2, *Ongoing Medical Information and Advice*, represents collaborative relationships between clinicians and families in which there is a steady flow of information both ways and a readiness to collaborate on decisions affecting the patient's and family's well-being. At this level, however, communication between clinicians and families is restricted to medical information and advice. Clinicians stick to the "facts" rather than also discussing the family's feelings about what is happening. Despite this limitation, we believe that many families would be delighted to have the free flow of information with clinicians that characterizes this level.

At Level 3, *Feelings and Support*, the clinician goes beyond the informational level and deals supportively with family members' emotional responses to what is happening. The clinician invites family members to share their fears and hopes, both concerning the patient and themselves. When the family is undergoing severe strain, the clinician can offer them emotional support, help them understand what is happening to them, and refer them, if appropriate, to support groups and other resources. We view this as an optimal level of involvement by primary care clinicians with families, one that most families under stress are open to and can benefit from, and one that also enhances the professional satisfaction of the clinician. At the same time, we recognize that time and other structural and institutional constraints may prevent these interactions from occurring as often as clinicians and families would like. Over an extended period of contact during a hospitalization, however, and certainly over a long-standing clinical relationship, Level 3 interactions are generally possible between motivated clinicians and families.

Level 4, *Systematic Assessment and Planned Intervention*, add to the previous levels the element of an intervention to help family members change their interaction patterns related to the illness. Such an intervention would likely occur only after Level 2 information exchanges and Level 3 emotional exchanges had occurred, with the family stuck in its effort to cope with the illness. For example, the family with a newly diagnosed adolescent diabetic may be experiencing conflict over responsibility for the insulin injections: The adolescent is saying "It's my responsibility," but is not complying with the regimen; and the parents are continually checking on the adolescent and criticizing her. The primary care clinician who is trained in the fundamentals of family systems theory and family interventions might assess the vicious circle the family is engaged in, and actively intervene in this family pattern, for example, by challenging the adolescent to follow through on her declarations of self-responsibility, while helping the parents move into an encouraging role that expects their daughter to take her injections, rather than a snooping and criticizing role that communicates lack of confidence in her.

Level 5, *Family Therapy*, represents intensive interventions into family systems that are rigidly dysfunctional. It requires training beyond what is normally available for primary care clinicians, except for those who take postgraduate training in family therapy. An ideal scenario would involve the close involvement of a family therapist in the clinical setting to work alongside primary care clinicians. In some cases, the therapist and clinician might work together with families who have particularly difficult biopsychosocial problems. But most often, when the primary care clinician assesses a serious family dysfunction, or when Level 3 or 4 involvement is not helpful in alleviating the problems, a referral is made to a Level 5 family therapist.

This model is intended as a guide to understanding the range of possibilities with families, rather than as a prescription about what the clinician should do with a particular family in a particular situation. Thus an interaction focused solely around medical information and advice might be most appropriate when the family does not want to discuss their feelings or when time is too short to open up potentially painful discussions. Likewise, Level 4 interventions are appropriate only when the family wants help with a problem; there must be a contract for psychosocial treatment just as there is for biomedical treatment. Thus the levels do not constitute a hierarchy of ideal treatment, but a delineation of the range of alternatives available to the clinician and the family. The levels also can be used as a way for the clinician to evaluate his or her competence in family-centered care, that is, how far along the levels can a clinician comfortably go. Some clinicians are comfortable only with facts, others can also handle emotional distress but do not know how to intervene. Finally, the model offers clinicians a guide to the personal development, knowledge, and skills they may wish to develop if they want to enhance their competency in working with families in health care.

As suggested by the foregoing discussion of multiple levels of family intervention, the full range of services needed by families is too large for any one clinician or any one profession to offer. Limitations imposed by time, training, and reimbursement mechanisms pose insurmountable obstacles to any clinician trying to be "all things" to families. The alternative is collaboration among professionals who have overlapping philosophies of health care but different training and work responsibilities. A model of such collaborative health care has been developed by Michael Glenn (1987). These arrangements challenge professionals to transcend their own traditions in search of improved services for families.

CONCLUSION

The 1980s have witnessed the flowering of interest in families and health among researchers and clinicians from a wide range of disciplines and professions. This growth has been fueled by the emergence of family medicine as a more mature discipline, by nursing's rediscovery of its commitment to the social context of patient care, and by the desire of family researchers and family therapists to understand families as biopsychosocial entities. Parallel developments in health psychology and in social and behavioral epidemiology have contributed strongly to the development of the family and health area.

At the same time, the 1980s have witnessed the beginnings of a radical transformation of the way health care is delivered in the United States, the reverberations from which will take many years to play themselves out. As economic forces and professional turf issues become increasingly salient considerations in the health care field, we hope that the work of the researchers and clinicians documented in this volume provides testimony to the importance of the family face of health care.

DISCUSSION QUESTIONS

(1) Discuss the advantages and limitations of the Family Health and Illness Cycle. What aspects of the family and health experience does it capture well? What aspects are not dealt with well in the model?
(2) Does family and health research seem more difficult or less difficult than other social science research? Is the area ripe for an overarching theory that might explain the relationship between families and health? If not, why?
(3) Discuss the advantages and disadvantages of each level of Doherty and Baird's Levels of Clinicians' Involvement with Families.

RECOMMENDED READINGS

Doherty, W. J., & Baird, M. A. (Eds.). (1987). *Family-centered medical care: A clinical casebook*. New York: Guilford.

Engel, G. L. (1977). The need for a new medical model: A challenge for biomedicine. *Science, 196*, 129-136.

Forman, B. D., & Hagan, B. J. (1983). A comparative review of total family functioning measures. *American Journal of Family Therapy, 11*, 25-40.

Litman, T. J., & Venters, M. (1979). Research on health care and the family: A methodological overview. *Social Science and Medicine, 13a*, 379-385.

References

Ablon, J. (1985). Irish-American Catholics in a West Coast metropolitan area. In L. A. Bennett & G. M. Ames (Eds.), *The American experience with alcohol: Contrasting cultural perspectives*. New York: Plenum.

Abramson, H. A., & Peshkin, H. M. (1979). Psychosomatic group therapy with parents of children with intractable asthma: The Peters family. *Journal of Asthma Research, 16,* 103-117.

Ader, R. (1981). *Psychoneuroimmunology.* New York: Academic Press.

Albert, J. J., Kosa, J., & Haggerty, R. J. (1967). A month of illness and health care among low-income families. *Public Health Reports, 82,* 705-713.

American Cancer Society. (1982). *Cancer facts and figures: 1983.* New York: Author.

American Heart Association. (1984). Recommendations for treatment of hyperlipidemias in adults: A joint statement of the Nutrition Committee and the Council on Arteriosclerosis. *Circulation, 65,* 839A-854A.

Anderson, B. J., & Auslander, W. F. (1980). Research on diabetes management and the family: A critique. *Diabetes Care, 3,* 696-702.

Anderson, B. J., Miller, J. P., Auslander, W. F., & Santiago, J. V. (1981). Family characteristics of diabetic adolescents: Relationship to metabolic control. *Diabetes Care, 4,* 586-594.

Antonovsky, A. (1979). *Health, stress, and coping.* San Francisco: Jossey-Bass.

Aries, P. (1975). The reversal of death: Changes in attitudes toward death in Western societies. In D. E. Stannard (Ed.), *Death in America*. Philadelphia: University of Pennsylvania Press.

Baker, L. C. (1987). Families and illness. In M. Crouch & L. Roberts (Eds.), *The family in medical practice: A family systems*. New York: Springer-Verlag.

Baker, L. C., Barcai, A., Kaye, R., & Haque, N. (1969). Beta adrenergic blockade and juvenile diabetes: Acute studies and long-term therapeutic trial. *Journal of Pediatrics, 75,* 19-29.

Baker, L. C., Minuchin, S., Milman, L., Liebman, R., & Todd, T. (1975). Psychosomatic aspects of juvenile diabetes mellitus: A progress report. *Modern Problems in Pediatrics, 12,* 332-343.

Baker, L. C., & Pontious, J. M. (1984). Treating the health care family. *Family Systems Medicine, 2,* 401-408.

Baranowski, T., & Nader, P. R. (1985). Family health behavior. In D. C. Turk & R. D. Kerns (Eds.), *Health, illness, and families: A life-span perspective*. New York: John Wiley.

Baranowski, T., Nader, P. R., Dunn, K., & Vanderpool, N. A. (1982, Summer). Family self-help: Promoting changes in health behavior. *Journal of Communications*, pp. 161-172.

Barbarin, O. A., & Chesler, M. A. (1984). Relationships with the medical staff and aspects of satisfaction with care expressed by parents of children with cancer. *Journal of Community Health, 9,* 302-312.

Barbarin, O. A., Hughes, D., & Chesler, M. A. (1985). Stress, coping, and marital functioning among parents of children with cancer. *Journal of Marriage and the Family, 47,* 473-480.

Barbarin, O. A., & Tirado, M. (1984). Family involvement and successful treatment of obesity: A review. *Family Systems Medicine, 2,* 37-45.

Bartrop, R. W., Luckhurst, E., Lazarus, L., Kiloh, L. G., & Penny, R. (1977). Depressed lymphocyte function after bereavement. *Lancet, 1,* 834-836.

Bass, L. W., & Cohen, R. I. (1982). Ostensible versus actual reasons for seeking pediatric attention: Another look at parental tickets of admission. *Pediatrics, 70,* 870-874.

Beautrais, A. L., Fergusson, D. M., & Shannon, F. T. (1982). Life events and childhood morbidity: A prospective study. *Pediatrics, 70,* 935-940.

Becker, L., Steinbauer, J., & Doherty, W. J. (1985). A biopsychosocial smoking cessation program. *Family Systems Medicine, 3,* 103-110.

Berkman, L. F. (1984). Assessing the physical health effects of social networks and social support. *Annual Review of Public Health, 5,* 413-432.

Berkman, L. F., & Syme, S. L. (1979). Social networks, host resistance and mortality: A nine year follow-up study of Alameda County residents. *American Journal of Epidemiology, 109,* 186-204.

Berlin, E. A., & Fowkes, W. C. (1983). A teaching framework for cross-cultural health care. *Western Journal of Medicine, 139,* 934-938.

Berman, S., & Villarreal, S. (1983). Use of a seminar as an aid in helping interns care for dying children and their families. *Clinical Pediatrics, 22,* 175-179.

von Bertalanffy, L. (1968). *General systems theory.* New York: Braziller.

Bewley, B. R., & Bland, J. M. (1977). Academic performance and social factors related to cigarette smoking by school children. *British Journal of Preventive and Social Medicine, 31,* 18-24.

Binger, C. M., Ablin, A. R., Geuerstein, R. C., Kushner, J. H., Zoger, S., & Mirrelsen, C. (1969). Childhood leukemia: Emotional impact on patient and family. *New England Journal of Medicine, 280,* 414-418.

Blazer, D. G. (1982). Social support and mortality in an elderly community population. *American Journal of Epidemiology, 115,* 684-694.

Borysenko, M., & Borysenko, J. (1982). Stress, behavior, and immunity: Animal models and mediating mechanisms. *General Hospital Psychiatry, 4,* 59-67.

Bowen, M. (1976). Family reaction to death. In P. Guerin (Ed.), *Family therapy.* New York: Gardner Press.

Boyce, W. T., Jensen, E. W., Cassel, J. C., Collier, A. M., Smith, A. H., & Ramey, C. T. (1977). Influence of life events and family routines on childhood respiratory illness. *Pediatrics, 60,* 609-615.

Breslau, N., Staruch, K. S., & Mortimer, E. A. (1982). Psychological distress in mothers of disabled children. *American Journal of Diseases of Children, 136,* 682-686.

Breslau, N., Weitzman, M., & Messenger, K. (1981). Psychologic functioning of siblings in disabled children. *Pediatrics, 67,* 344-353.

Broadhead, W. E., Kaplan, B. H., James, S. A., Wagner, E. H., Schoenback, V. J., Grimson, R., Heyden, S., Tibblin, G., & Gehlback, S. H. (1983). The epidemiologic evidence for a relationship between social support and health. *American Journal of Epidemiology, 117,* 521-537.

Brody, S. J., Poulshock, S. W., & Masciocchi, C. F. (1978). The family caring unit: A major consideration in the long-term support system. *Gerontologist, 18,* 556-561.

Brownell, K. D., Heckerman, C. L., Westlake, R. J., Hayes, S. C., & Monti, P. M. (1978). The effects of couples training and partner co-operativeness in the behavioral treatment of obesity. *Behavioral Research and Therapy, 16,* 323-333.

Brownell, K. D., Kelman, J. H., & Stunkard, A. J. (1983). Treatment of obese children with and without their mothers: Changes in weight and blood pressure. *Pediatrics, 71,* 515-523.

Bruhn, J. G. (1977). Effects of chronic illness on the family. *Journal of Family Practice, 4,* 1057-1060.

Bryan, M. S., & Lowenberg, M. E. (1958). The father's influence on young children's food preferences. *Journal of American Dietetic Association, 34,* 30-35.

Bunch, J., Barraclough, B., Nelson, B., & Sainsbury, P. (1971). Suicide following death of parents. *Social Psychiatry, 6,* 193-199.

Burr, W. R., Hill, R., Nye, F. I., & Reiss, I. L. (Eds.). (1979). *Contemporary theories about the family* (2 vols.). New York: Free Press.

Cairns, N. U., Clark, G. M., Smith, S. D., & Lansky, S. B. (1979). Adaptation of siblings to childhood malignancy. *Journal of Pediatrics, 95,* 484-487.

Caldwell, R., Cobb, S., Dowling, M. D., & Jongh, D. (1970). The dropout problem in antihypertensive therapy. *Journal of Chronic Diseases, 22,* 579-592.

Califano, J.A.J. (1979). *Healthy people: The Surgeon General's report on health promotion and disease prevention,* DHEW (PHS) Publication No. 79-55071. Public Health Service. Washington, DC: Government Printing Office.

Campbell, T. L. (1985). Family's impact on health: A critical review and annotated bibliography. *Family Systems Medicine, 4,* 135-328.

Campbell, T. L. (1986). *Family's impact on health: A critical review and annotated bibliography,* National Institute of Mental Health Series DN No. 6, DHHS Pub. No. (ADM) 86-1461. Washington, DC: Government Printing Office.

Candib, L. M., Steinberg, S. L., Bedinghaus, J., Martin, M., Wheeler, R., Pugnaire, M., & Wertheimer, R. (1987). Doctors having families: The effect of pregnancy and childbearing on relationships with patients. *Family Medicine, 19,* 114-119.

Carter, H., & Glick, P. C. (1970). *Marriage and divorce: A social and economic study.* Cambridge, MA: Harvard University Press.

Carter, R. E. (1984). Family reactions and reorganization patterns in myocardial infarction. *Family Systems Medicine, 2,* 55-65.

Cassel, J. (1976). The contribution of the social environment to host resistance. *American Journal of Epidemiology, 104,* 107-123.

Cassem, N. H., & Stewart, R. S. (1975). Management and care of the dying patient. *International Journal of Psychiatry in Medicine, 6,* 293-302.

Cassileth, B. R., Lusk, E. J., Strouse, T. B., Miller, D. S., Brown, L. L., & Cross, P. A. (1985). A psychological analysis of cancer patients and their next of kin. *Cancer, 55,* 72-76.

Cederblad, M., Helgesson, M., Larsson, Y., & Ludvigsson, J. (1982). Family structure and diabetes in children. *Pediatric Adolescent Endocrinology, 10,* 94-98.

Center for Disease Control. (1986). *Smoking and health: A national status report,* DHHS Pub. No. (CDC) 87-8396. Rockville, MD: Public Health Service.

Christensen, H. (Ed.). (1964). *Handbook of marriage and the family.* Chicago: Rand McNally.

Christie-Seely, J. (Ed.). (1984). *Working with families in primary care.* New York: Praeger.

Clayton, P. (1974). Mortality and morbidity in the first year of widowhood. *Archives of General Psychiatry, 30,* 747-750.

Clayton, P. (1979). The sequelae and nonsequelae of conjugal bereavement. *American Journal of Psychiatry, 136,* 1530-1534.

Cluff, L. (1981). Chronic disease, function and the quality of care [Editorial]. *Journal of Chronic Disease, 34,* 299-304.

Cobb, S., Harburg, E., Tabor, J., Hunt, P., Kasl, S. V., & Schull, W. J. (1969). The intrafamilial transmission of rheumatoid arthritis. *Journal of Chronic Disease, 22,* 193-194.

Cogswell, B. E., & Sussman, M. B. (Eds.). (1981). *Family medicine: A new approach to health care.* New York: Haworth.

Cohen, F. (1981). Stress and bodily illness. *Psychiatric Clinics of North America, 4,* 269-285.

Cohen, I. B. (1985). *Revolution in science.* Cambridge, MA: Harvard University Belknap Press.

Cohen, S., & Syme, S. L. (Eds.). (1985). *Social support and health.* Orlando, FL: Academic Press.

Combrinck-Graham, L. (1985). A developmental model for family system. *Family Process, 24,* 139-150.

Conrad, P. (1985). The meaning of medications: Another look at compliance. *Social Science and Medicine, 20,* 29-37.

Coppotelli, H. C., & Orleans, C. T. (1985). Partner support and other determinants of smoking cessation maintenance among women. *Journal of Consulting and Clinical Psychology, 53,* 455-460.

Council on Scientific Affairs. (1983). Dietary and pharmacologic therapy for lipid risk factors. *Journal of the American Medical Association, 250,* 1873-1879.

Crain, A. J., Sussman, M. B., & Weil, W. B. (1966). Effects of a diabetic child on marital integration and related measures of family functioning. *Journal of Health and Human Behavior, 7,* 122-127.

Culpepper, L., & Becker, L. A. (1987). *Family medicine research: Developing its base. In W. J. Doherty, C. E. Christianson, & M. B. Sussman (Eds.), Family medicine: The maturing of a discipline.* New York: Haworth.

Dano, P., & Hahn-Pedersen, J. (1977). Improvement in quality of life following jejunoileal bypass surgery for morbid obesity. *Scandinavian Journal of Gastroenterology, 12,* 769-774.

Demers, R. Y., Altamore, R., Mustin, H., Kleinman, A., & Leonardi, D. (1980). An exploration of the dimensions of illness behavior. *Journal of Family Practice, 11,* 1085-1092.

Dever, G.E.A. (1980). *Community health analysis: A holistic approach.* Germantown, MD: Aspen.

Doane, J. A., Falloon, R. H., Goldstein, M. J., & Mintz, J. (1985). Parental affective style and the treatment of schizophrenia: Predicting course of illness and social functioning. *Archives of General Psychiatry, 42,* 34-42.

Doherty, W. J. (1985). Family interventions in health care. *Family Relations, 34,* 129-137.

Doherty, W. J. (1986). Family therapy in family medicine. In A. S. Gurman & N. S. Jacobson (Eds.), *Clinical handbook of marital therapy.* New York: Guilford.

Doherty, W. J., & Baird, M. A. (1983). *Family therapy and family medicine: Toward the primary care of families.* New York: Guilford.

Doherty, W. J., & Baird, M. A. (1984). A protocol for family compliance counseling. *Family Systems Medicine, 2,* 333-336.

Doherty, W. J., & Baird, M. A. (1986). Developmental levels in family-centered medical care. *Family Medicine, 18,* 153-156.

Doherty, W. J., & Baird, M. A. (Eds.). (1987). *Family-centered medical care: A clinical casebook.* New York: Guilford.

Doherty, W. J., Baird, M. A., & Becker, L. A. (1987). Family medicine and the biopsychosocial model: The road toward integration. In W. J. Doherty, C. Christianson, & M. B. Sussman (Eds.), *Family medicine: The maturing of a discipline.* New York: Haworth.

Doherty, W. J., Christianson, C. E., & Sussman, M. B. (Eds.). (1987). *Family medicine: The maturing of a discipline.* New York: Haworth.

Doherty, W. J., & Colangelo, N. (1984). The family FIRO model: A modest proposal for organizing family treatment. *Journal of Marital and Family Therapy, 10,* 19-29.

Doherty, W. J., Colangelo, N., Green, A. M., & Hoffman, G. S. (1985). Emphasis of the major family therapy models: A family FIRO analysis. *Journal of Marital and Family Therapy, 11,* 299-303.

Doherty, W. J., & McCubbin, H. I. (1985). The family and health care [Special issue]. *Family Relations, 34,* 1.

Doherty, W. J., Schrott, H. G., Metcalf, L., & Iassiello-Vailas, L. (1983). Effect of spouse support and health beliefs on medication adherence. *Journal of Family Practice, 17,* 837-841.

Doherty, W. J., & Whitehead, D. (1986). The social dynamics of cigarette smoking: A family systems perspective. *Family Process, 25,* 453-460.

Dunbar, J., & Stunkard, A. J. (1979). Adherence to diet and drug regimen. In R. Levey, B. Rifkin, B. Dennis, & N. Ernst (Eds.), *Nutrition, lipids, and coronary heart disease.* New York: Raven.

Earp, J. L., Ory, M. G., & Strogatz, D. S. (1982). The effects of family involvement and practitioner home visits on the control of hypertension. *American Journal of Public Health, 72,* 1146-1153.

Eaustaugh, S. R., & Hatcher, M. E. (1982). Improving compliance among hypertensives: A triage criterion with cost benefit implications. *Medical Care, 20,* 1001-1017.

Eisenberg, L., & Kleinman, A. (1981). *The relevance of social science for medicine.* Boston, MA: D. Reidel.

Engel, G. L. (1971). Sudden and rapid death during psychological stress: Folk lore or folk wisdom. *Annuals of Internal Medicine, 74,* 771-782.

Engel, G. L. (1977). The need for a new medical model: A challenge for biomedicine. *Science, 196,* 129-136.

Epstein, N. B., Bishop, D. S., & Levin, S. (1978). The McMaster model of family functioning. *Journal of Marriage and Family Counseling, 4,* 19-31.

Falloon, I. R., Boyd, J. L., & McGill, C. W. (1984). *Family care of schizophrenia.* New York: Guilford.

Falloon, I. R., Boyd, J. L., McGill, C. W., Razani, J., Moss, H. B., & Gilderman, A. M. (1982). Family management in the prevention of exacerbations of schizophrenia: A controlled study. *New England Journal of Medicine, 306,* 1437-1440.

Feinleib, M., Garrison, R. J., Fabsitz, R. et al. (1977). The NHLBI twin study of cardiovascular disease risk factors: Methodology and summary of results. *American Journal of Epidemiology, 106,* 284-295.

Ferrari, M., Matthews, W. S., & Barabas, G. (1983). The family and the child with epilepsy. *Family Process, 22*, 53-59.

Fielding, J. E. (1985). Smoking: Health effects and control. *NEJM, 313*, 491-498, 555-561.

Fink, S. L., Skipper, J. K., & Hallenbeck, P. N. (1968). Physical disability and problems in marriage. *Journal of Marriage and the Family, 30*, 64-73.

Fischer, A. E., & Dolger, H. (1946). Behavior and psychological problems of young diabetic patients. *Archives of Internal Medicine, 78*, 711-732.

Flora, G. G. (1977). Problem solving in diagnostics and therapeutic of neurology: The treatment of seizure disorders. *South Dakota Journal of Medicine, 30*, 15-16.

Fogarty, T. F. (1979). The distance and pursuer. *The Family, 7*, 11-16.

Forman, B. D., & Hagan, B. J. (1983). A comparative review of total family functioning measures. *American Journal of Family Therapy, 11*, 25-40.

Friel, P. B. (1983). Death and dying. *Annals of Internal Medicine, 97*, 767-771.

Gardner, R. (1969). The guilt reaction of parents of children with severe physical disease. *American Journal of Psychiatry, 126*, 636-644.

Garn, S. M., Cole, P. E., & Bailey, S. M. (1976). Effect of parental fatness levels on the fatness of biological and adoptive children. *Ecology of Food and Nutrition, 6*, 1-3.

Gilder, R., Buschman, P. R., Sitarz, A. L., & Wolff, J. A. (1978). Group therapy with parents of children with leukemia. *American Journal of Psychotherapy, 32*, 276-286.

Gilliss, C. L., Highley, B. L., Roberts, B. M., & Martinson, I. M. (In press). *Toward a science of family nursing*. Connecticut: Appleton-Canger.

Glazier, W. (1973). The task of medicine. *Scientific American, 228*, 13-17.

Glenn, M. L. (1984). *On diagnosis: A systemic approach*. New York: Brunner/Mazel.

Glenn, M. L. (1987). *Collaborative health care: A family-oriented approach*. New York: Praeger.

Golub, E. (1981). Cancer and death in the Promethean Age. *Journal of Popular Culture, 14*, 725-731.

Gorton, T. A., Doerfler, D. L., Hulka, B. S., & Tyroler, H. A. (1979). Intrafamilial patterns of illness reports and physician visits in a community sample. *Journal of Health and Social Behavior, 20*, 37-44.

Gottlieb, B. H. (1976). Lay influences on the utilization and provision of health services: A review. *Canadian Psychological Review, 17*, 126-136.

Graham, S., & Gibson, R. W. (1971). Cessation of patterned behavior: Withdrawal from smoking. *Social Science and Medicine, 5*, 319-337.

Grey, M. J., Genel, M., & Tamborlane, W. V. (1980). Psychosocial adjustment of latency-age diabetics: Determinants and relationship to control. *Pediatrics, 65*, 69-73.

Haley, J. (1980). *Leaving home*. New York: McGraw-Hill.

Hartman, A., & Laird, J. (1983). *Family-centered social work practice*. New York: Free Press.

Hartz, A., Giefer, E., & Rimm, A. A. (1977). Relative importance of the effect of family environment and heredity on obesity. *Annual of Human Genetics, 41*, 185-193.

Hauck, G. (1972). Sociological aspects of epilepsy research. *Epilepsia, 13*, 79-85.

Haynes, R. B., Mattson, M. E., Chobanian, A. V., Dunbar, J. M., Engebretson, T. O. et al. (1982). Management of patient compliance in the treatment of hypertension: Report of the NHLBI working group. *Hypertension, 4*, 415-423.

Haynes, R. B., Taylor, D. W., & Sackett, D. L. (Eds.). (1979). *Compliance in health care*. Baltimore: Johns Hopkins University Press.

Heinzelman, F., & Bagley, R. W. (1970). Response to physical activity programs and their effects on health behavior. *Public Health Reports, 85,* 905-911.

Helsing, K. J., & Szklo, M. (1981). Mortality after bereavement. *American Journal of Epidemiology, 114,* 41-52.

Henao, S., & Grose, N. P. (Eds.). (1985). *Principles of family systems in family medicine.* New York: Brunner/Mazel.

Hepworth, J., & Jackson, M. (1985). Health care for families: Models of collaboration between family therapist and family physicians. *Family Relations, 34,* 123-127.

Hilfiker, D. (1984). Facing our mistakes. *New England Journal of Medicine, 310,* 118-122.

Hill, R. (1949). *Families under stress.* New York: Harper.

Hill, R. (1958). Generic features of families under stress. *Social Casework, 39,* 139-159.

Hoebel, F. C. (1976). Brief family-interactional therapy in the management of cardiac-related high-risk behaviors. *Journal of Family Practice, 3,* 613-618.

Hofer, M. A. (1984). Relationships as regulators: A psychobiologic perspective on bereavement. *Psychosomatic Medicine, 46,* 183-197.

Hollingsworth, C. E., & Pasnau, R. O. (1977). The physician's responsibility. Pp. 41-44 in C. E. Hollingsworth & R. O. Pasnau (Eds.), *The family in mourning: A guide for health professionals.* New York: Grune & Stratton.

Holmes, T. H., & Rahe, R. H. (1967). The social readjustment scale. *Journal of Psychosomatic Research, 39,* 413-431.

House, J. S., Robbins, C., & Metzner, H. L. (1982). The association of social relationships and activities with mortality: Prospective evidence from the Tecumseh Community Health Study. *American Journal of Epidemiology, 116,* 123-140.

Irvine, P. (1985). The attending at the funeral. *New England Journal of Medicine, 312,* 1704-1705.

Isaacs, B. (1971). Geriatric patients: Do their families care? *British Medical Journal, 4,* 282-286.

Jacobs, S., & Ostfeld, A. (1977). An epidemiological review of the mortality of bereavement. *Psychosomatic Medicine, 39,* 344-357.

Jemmott, J. B., & Locke, S. E. (1984). Psychosocial factors, immunologic mediation, and human susceptibility to infectious diseases: How much do we know? *Psychological Bulletin, 95,* 78-108.

Johnson, E. M., & Stark, D. E. (1980). A group program for cancer patients and their family members in an acute care teaching hospital. *Social Work in Health Care, 5,* 335-349.

Johnson, S. B. (1980). Psychosocial factors in juvenile diabetes: A review. *Journal of Behavioral Medicine, 3,* 95-116.

Kalnins, I. V., Churchill, M. P., & Terry, G. E. (1980). Concurrent stress in families with a leukemic child. *Journal of Pediatric Psychology, 5,* 81-92.

Kasl, S. V., & Cobb, S. (1966). Health behavior, illness behavior, and sick role behavior. *Archives of Environmental Health, 12,* 246-266.

Khurana, R., & White, P. (1970). Attitudes of the diabetic child and his parents towards his illness. *Postgraduate Medicine, 48,* 72-76.

Klein, R. F., Dean, A., & Bogdonoff, M. D. (1967). The impact of illness on the spouse. *Journal of Chronic Disease, 20,* 241-248.

Kleinman, A. (1980). *Patients and healers in the context of culture.* Berkeley: University of California Press.

Klus, J., Habbick, B. F., & Abernathy, T. J. (1983). Diabetes in children: Family responses and control. *Psychosomatics, 24,* 367-372.

Koch, A. (1985). "If only it could be me": The families of pediatric cancer patients. *Family Relations, 34,* 63-70.

Komarovsky, M. (1940). *The unemployed man and his family.* New York: Dryden.

Kones, R. J. (1979). Emotional stress, plasma catecholamines, cardiac risk factors, and atherosclerosis. *Angiology, 30,* 327-336.

Korsch, B. M., & Negrette, V. F. (1972). Doctor-patient communication. *Scientific American, 227,* 66-74.

Koski, M. L., & Kumenta, A. (1977). The interrelationship between diabetic control and family life. *Pediatric Adolescent Endocrinology, 3,* 41-45.

Koukal, S. M., & Parham, E. S. (1978). A family learning experience to serve the juvenile patient with diabetes. *Journal of American Diabetic Association, 72,* 411-413.

Krant, M. J., Doster, N. J., & Ploof, S. (1980). Meeting the needs of the late-stage elderly cancer patient and family: A clinical model. *Journal of Geriatric Psychiatry, 13,* 53-61.

Krant, M. J., & Johnston, L. (1978). Family member's perception of communication in late-stage cancer. *International Journal of Psychiatry in Medicine, 8,* 203-216.

Kraus, A. S., & Lilienfeld, A. M. (1959). Some epidemiological aspects of the high mortality rate in the young widowed group. *Journal of Chronic Disease, 10,* 207-217.

Kübler-Ross, E. (1969). *On death and dying.* New York: Macmillan.

Kucia, C., Drotar, D., Doershuk, C., Stern, R., Boat, T., & Matthews, L. (1979). Home observations of family interaction and childhood adjustment to cystic fibrosis. *Journal of Pediatric Psychology, 4,* 189-195.

Kuzel, A. J. (1986). Naturalistic inquiry: An appropriate model for family medicine. *Family Medicine, 18,* 369-374.

Lansky, S. B., Cairns, N. U., Hassanein, Wehr, J., & Lowman, J. T. (1978). Childhood cancer: Parental discord and divorce. *Pediatrics, 62,* 184-188.

Lave, J. R. (1985). Cost containment polices in long-term care. *Inquiry, 22,* 7-23.

Lavigne, J. V., & Ryan, M. (1979). Psychologic adjustment of siblings of children with chronic illness. *Pediatrics, 63,* 616-627.

Leff, J., Kuipers, L., Berkowitz, R., Everlein-Vries, R., & Sturgeon, D. (1982). A controlled trial of social interventions in the families of schizophrenic patients. *British Journal of Psychiatry, 141,* 121-134.

Leventhal, H., Leventhal, E. A., & Van Nguyen, T. (1985). Reactions of families to illness: Theoretical models and perspectives. In D. C. Turk & R. D. Kerns (Eds.), *Health, illness, and families: A life-span perspective.* New York: John Wiley.

Levine, D. M., Green, L. W., Deeds, S. G., Chwalow, J., Russel, R. P., & Finlay, J. (1979). Health education for hypertensive patients. *Journal of the American Medical Association, 241,* 1700-1703.

Lewis, J. M., Beavers, W. R., Gossett, J. T., & Philips, V. A. (1976). *No single thread.* New York: Brunner-Mazel.

Lichtenstein, E. (1982). The smoking problem: A behavioral perspective. *Journal of Consulting and Clinical Psychology, 50,* 465-466.

Like, R. C., & Steiner, R. P. (1986). Medical anthropology and the family physician. *Family Medicine, 18,* 87-92.

Lindemann, E. (1944). Symptomatology and management of acute grief. *American Journal of Psychiatry, 101,* 500-541.

Lipowski, Z. J. (1969). Psychosocial aspects of disease. *Annals of Internal Medicine, 71,* 1197-1206.

Litman, T. J. (1974). The family as a basic unit in health and medical care: A social-behavioral overview. *Social Science and Medicine, 8,* 495-519.

Litman, T. J., & Venters, M. (1979). Research on health care and the family: A methodological overview. *Social Science and Medicine, 13A,* 379-385.

Locke, H. J., & Wallace, K. M. (1959). Short-term marital adjustment and prediction tests: Their reliability and validity. *Journal of Marriage and Family Living, 21,* 251-255.

Lown, B., Desilva, R. A., Reich, P., & Murawski, B. J. (1980). Psychophysiologic factors in sudden cardiac death. *American Journal of Psychiatry, 137,* 1325-1335.

Lubkin, I. M. (1986). *Chronic illness: Impact and interventions.* Boston: Jones & Bartlett.

Lynch, J. (1977). *The broken heart: The medical consequences of loneliness.* New York: Basic Books.

MacMahon, B., & Pugh, T. F. (1965). Suicide in the widowed. *American Journal of Epidemiology, 81,* 23-31.

Marrero, D. G., Lau, N., Golden, M. P., Kershnar, A., & Myers, G. C. (1982). Family dynamics in adolescent diabetes mellitus: Parental behavior and metabolic control. *Pediatric Adolescent Endocrinology, 10,* 77-82.

Marshall, J. R., & Neill, F. (1977). The removal of a psychosomatic symptom: Effects on the marriage. *Family Process, 16,* 273-280.

Marten, G. W., & Mauer, A. M. (1982). Interaction of health-care professionals with critically ill children and their parents. *Clinical Pediatrics, 21,* 540-544.

Matarazzo, J. D. (1984). Behavioral health: A 1990 challenge for the health sciences professions. In J. D. Matarazzo, S. M. Weiss, J. A. Herd, N. E. Miller, & S. M. Weiss (Eds.), *Behavioral health: A handbook of health enhancement and disease prevention.* New York: John Wiley.

Maurin, J., & Schenkel, J. (1976). A study of the family unit's response to hemodialysis. *Journal of Psychosomatic Research, 20,* 163-168.

McCubbin, H. I., Joy, C. B., Cauble, A. E., Comeau, J. K., Patterson, J. M., & Needle, R. H. (1980). Family stress and coping: A decade review. *Journal of Marriage and the Family, 42,* 855-871.

McCubbin, H. I., & Patterson, J. M. (1983). The family stress process: The double ABCX model of adjustment and adaptation. In H. I. McCubbin, M. B. Sussman, & J. M. Patterson (Eds.), *Social stress and the family: Advances and developments in family stress theory and research.* New York: Haworth.

McDaniel, S. H., Bank, J., Campbell, T., Mancini, J., & Shore, B. (1986). Using group as a consultant: A systems approach to medical care. In L. C. Wynne, S. H. McDaniel, & T. Weber (Eds.), *Systems consultation: A new perspective for family therapy.* New York: Guilford.

McKenney, J. M., Slining, J. M., Henderson, H. R., Devins, D., & Barr, M. (1973). The effect of clinical pharmacy services on patients with essential hypertension. *Circulation, 48,* 1104-1111.

Medalie, J. H., & Goldbourt, U. (1976). Angina pectoris among 10,000 men: Psychosocial and other risk factors as evidenced by a multivariate analysis of a five year incidence study. *American Journal of Medicine, 60,* 910-921.

Mermelstein, R., Lichtenstein, E., & McIntyre, K. (1983). Partner support and relapse in smoking cessation programs. *Journal of Consulting and Clinical Psychology, 51,* 465-466.

Meyer, R. J., & Haggerty, R. J. (1962). Streptococcal infections in families: Factors altering individual susceptibility. *Pediatrics, 29,* 539-549.

Minuchin, S., Baker, L., Rosman, B. L., Liebman, R., Milman, L., & Todd, T. C. (1975). A conceptual model of psychosomatic illness in children: Family organization and family therapy. *Archives of General Psychiatry, 32,* 1031-1038.

Minuchin, S., Rosman, B. L., & Baker, L. (1978). *Psychosomatic families: Anorexia nervosa in context.* Cambridge, MA: Harvard University Press.

Moos, R. H. (1974). *The social climate scales: An overview.* Palo Alto: Consulting Psychologists Press.

Moos, R. H., & Moos, B. S. (1976). A typology of family social environments. *Family Process, 15,* 357-371.

Morisky, D. E., Levine, D. M., Green, L. W., Shapiro, S., Russell, R. P., & Smith, C. R. (1983). Five year blood pressure control and mortality following health education for hypertensive patients. *American Journal of Public Health, 73,* 153-162.

Murphy, G., & Robins, E. (1967). Social factors in suicide. *Journal of the American Medical Association, 199,* 303-308.

National Center for Health Statistics. (1984). *Health, United States,* DHHS Pub. No. (PHS) 85-1232. Public Health Service. Washington, DC: Government Printing Office.

National Center for Health Statistics. (1986). *Health promotion data for the 1990 objectives,* No. 126. DHHS Pub. No. (PHS) 86-1250. Washington, DC: Government Printing Office.

National Heart, Lung, and Blood Institute. (1982). Management of patient compliance in the treatment of hypertension. *Hypertension, 4,* 415-423.

Neser, W. B., Tyroler, H. A., & Cassel, J. C. (1971). Social disorganization and stroke mortality in the Black population of North Carolina. *American Journal of Epidemiology, 93,* 166-175.

Newacheck, P. W., & Halfon, N. (1986). The association between mother's and children's use of physician services. *Medical Care, 24,* 30-38.

Newman, M. A. (1983). A continuing revolution: A history of nursing science. In N. L. Cvhaska (Ed.), *A time to speak.* New York: McGraw-Hill.

Nolte, A. E., Smith, B. J., & O'Rourke, T. (1983). The relationship between health risk attitudes and behavior upon youth smoking behavior. *Journal of School Health, 53,* 234-240.

Norbeck, J. S., & Tilden, V. P. (1983). Life stress, social supports, and emotional disequilibrium in complications of pregnancy: A prospective, multivariate study. *Journal of Health and Social Behavior, 24,* 30-46.

Northouse, L. (1984). The impact of cancer on the family: An overview. *International Journal of Psychiatry in Medicine, 14,* 215-242.

Nuckolls, K. B., Cassel, J., & Kaplan, B. H. (1972). Psychosocial assets, life crisis and the prognosis of pregnancy. *American Journal of Epidemiology, 95,* 431-441.

Oberst, M. T., & James, R. H. (1985, April). Going home: Patient and spouse adjustment following cancer surgery. *Topics in Clinical Nursing,* pp. 46-57.

O'Brien, R. (1986, August 7). *Role of social support during the first year of bereavement.* Paper presented at the Department of Family Medicine Grand Rounds, Rochester, New York.

Ockene, J. K., Nuttall, R. L., Benfari, R. S. et al. (1981). A psychosocial model of smoking cessation and maintenance of cessation. *Preventive Medicine, 10,* 623-638.

Oliveri, M. E., & Reiss, D. (1984). Family concepts and their measurement: Things are seldom what they seem. *Family Process, 23,* 33-48.

Olsen, J. (1970). The impact of serious illness on the family system. *Postgraduate Medicine, 47,* 169-174.

Olson, D. H. (1986). Circumplex model VII: Validation studies and FACES III. *Family Process, 25,* 337-351.

Olson, D. H., Portner, J., & Lavee, Y. (1985). *FACES III.* St. Paul: University of Minnesota, Family Social Science.

Olson, D. H., Sprenkle, D. H., & Russel, C. S. (1979). Circumplex model of marital and family systems: I. Cohesion and adaptability dimensions, family types, and clinical applications. *Family Process, 18,* 3-28.

Orr, D. P., Golden, M. P., Myers, G., & Marrerro, D. G. (1983). Characteristics of adolescents with poorly controlled diabetes referred to a tertiary care center. *Diabetes Care, 6,* 170-175.

Osterweis, M., Bush, P. J., & Zuckerman, A. E. (1979). Family context as a predictor of individual medicine use. *Social Sciences and Medicine, 13A,* 287-291.

Osterweis, M., Solomon, F., & Green, M. (Eds.). (1984). *Bereavement: Reactions, consequences, and care.* Washington, DC: National Academy Press.

Parkes, C. M. (1964). Effects of bereavement on physical and mental health: A study of the medical records of widows. *British Medical Journal, 2,* 274-279.

Parkes, C. M., Benjamin, B., & Fitzgerald, R. G. (1969). Broken heart: A statistical study of increased mortality among widowers. *British Medical Journal, 1,* 740-743.

Parkes, C. M., & Brown, R. J. (1972). Health after bereavement: A controlled study of young Boston widows and widowers. *Psychosomatic Medicine, 34,* 449-461.

Parkes, C. M., & Weiss, R. S. (1983). *Recovery from bereavement.* New York: Basic Books.

Pasnau, R. O., & Hollingsworth, C. E. (1977). Mourning in the health care team. In C. E. Hollingsworth & R. O. Pasnau (Eds.), *The family in mourning: A guide for health professionals.* New York: Grune & Stratton.

Patterson, J. M., & McCubbin, H. I. (1983). Chronic illness: Family stress and coping. In C. R. Figley & H. I. McCubbin (Eds.), *Stress and the family: Vol. 2. Coping with catastrophe.* New York: Brunner/Mazel.

Paykel, E. S., Myers, J. K., Dienelt, M. N., & Klerman, G. L. (1969). Life events and depression: A controlled trial. *Archives of General Psychiatry, 21,* 753-760.

Pearce, J. W., LeBow, M. D., & Orchard, J. (1981). Role of spouse involvement in the behavioral treatment of overweight women. *Journal of Consulting and Clinical Psychology, 49,* 236-244.

Pearlin, L. I., Menaghan, E. G., Lieberman, M. A., & Mullan, J. T. (1981). The stress process. *Journal of Health and Social Behavior, 22,* 337-365.

Penn, P. (1983). Coalitions and binding interactions in families with chronic illness. *Family Systems Medicine, 1,* 16-25.

Pless, I. B., & Satterwhite, B. B. (1973). A measure of family functioning and its application. *Social Science and Medicine, 7,* 613-621.

Pratt, L. (1976). Family structure and effective health behavior: The energized family. Boston: Houghton-Mifflin.

Price, R. A., Chen, K. H., Cavalli, S. L. et al. (1981). Models of spouse influence and their applications to smoking behavior. *Social Biology, 28,* 14-29.

Rabkin, J. G., & Struening, E. L. (1976). Life events, stress and illness. *Science, 194,* 1013-1020.

Ransom, D. C. (1981). The rise of family medicine: New roles for behavioral science. *Marriage and Family Review, 4,* 31-72.

Rand, C.S.W., Kuldau, J. M., & Robbins, L. (1982). Surgery for obesity and marriage quality. *Journal of the American Medical Association, 247,* 1419-1422.

Reiss, D. (1981). *The family's construction of reality.* Cambridge, MA: Harvard University Press.

Reiss, D., Gonzalez, S., & Kramer, N. (1986). Family process, chronic illness, and death. *Archives of General Psychiatry, 43,* 795-804.

Ritchie, K. (1981). Research note: Interaction in the families of epileptic children. *Journal of Child Psychology and Psychiatry, 22,* 65-71.

Robach, H. B. (Ed.). (1984). *Helping patients and their families cope with medical problems.* San Francisco: Jossey-Bass.

Roghmann, K. J., & Haggerty, R. J. (1973). Daily stress, illness, and use of health services in young families. *Pediatric Research, 7,* 520-526.

Rolland, J. S. (1984). Toward a psychosocial typology of chronic and life threatening illness. *Family Systems Medicine, 2,* 245-262.

Rolland, J. S. (1987). Chronic illness and the life cycle: A conceptual framework. *Family Process, 26,* 203-222.

Ross, J. L., & Phipps, E. (1986). Physician-patient power struggles: Their role in noncompliance. *Family Medicine, 18,* 99-101.

Ruberman, W., Weinblatt, E., Goldberg, J. D., & Chaudhary, B. S. (1984). Psychosocial influences on mortality after myocardial infarction. *New England Journal of Medicine, 311,* 552-559.

Sabbeth, B. (1984). Understanding the impact of chronic illness on families. *Pediatric Clinics of North America, 31,* 47-57.

Sabbeth, B., & Leventhal, J. M. (1984). Marital adjustment to chronic childhood illness: A critique of the literature. *Pediatrics, 73,* 762-768.

Saccone, A. J., & Israel, A. C. (1978). Effects of experimental versus significant other-controlled reinforcement and choice of target behavior on weight loss. *Behavior Therapy, 9,* 271-278.

Sackett, D. L., Anderson, G. D., Milner, R., Feinleib, M., & Kannel, W. B. (1975). Concordance for coronary risk factors among spouses. *Circulation, 52,* 589-595.

Sargent, A. J. (1983). The sick child and the family. *Journal of Pediatrics, 102,* 982-987.

Schaffer, H. R. (1964). The too cohesive family: A form of group pathology. *International Journal of Social Psychology, 10,* 266-275.

Schleifer, S. J., Keller, S. E., Camerino, M., Thornton, J. C., & Stein, M. (1983). Suppression of lymphocyte stimulation following bereavement. *Journal of the American Medical Association, 250,* 374-377.

Schutz, W. C. (1958). *FIRO: A three dimensional theory of interpersonal behavior.* New York: Holt, Rinehart & Winston.

Shouval, R., Ber, R., & Galatzer, A. (1982). Family social climate and the health status and social adaptation of diabetic youth. *Pediatric Adolescent Endocrinology, 10,* 89-93.

Silverman, P. R. (1970). The widow as caregiver in a program of preventive intervention with other widows. *Mental Hygiene, 54,* 540-547.

Singer, M. T., & Wynne, L. C. (1965a). Thought disorder and family relations of schizophrenia: III. Methodology using projective techniques. *Archives of General Psychiatry, 12,* 187-200.

Singer, M. T., & Wynne, L. C. (1965b). Thought disorder and family relations of schizophrenia: IV. Results and implications. *Archives of General Psychiatry, 12,* 201-212.

Solow, C., & Silberfarb, P.M.S.K. (1974). Psychosocial effects of intestinal bypass surgery for severe obesity. *New England Journal of Medicine, 290,* 300-304.

Stanton, M. D., & Todd, T. C. (1982). *The family therapy of drug abuse and addiction.* New York: Guilford.

Starr, P. (1982). *The social transformation of American medicine.* New York: Basic Books.

Steinglass, P., Temple, S., Lisman, S., & Reiss, D. (1982). Coping with spinal cord injury: The family perspective. *General Hospital Psychiatry, 4,* 259-264.

Strickland, R., Allstrom, J., & Davidson, J. (1981). The negative influence of families on compliance. *Hospital and Community Psychiatry, 5,* 349-350.

Stuart, R. B., & Davis, B. (1972). *Slim chance in a fat world: Behavioral control of obesity.* Champaign, IL: Research Press.

Stunkard, A. J., Sorensen, T.I.A., Hanis, C. et al. (1986). An adoption study of human obesity. *New England Journal of Medicine, 314,* 193-201.

Susser, M. (1981). Widowhood: A situational life stressor or a stressful life event. *American Journal of Public Health, 71,* 793-795.

Sussman, M. B. (1976). The family life of old people. In R. H. Binstock & E. Shanas (Eds.), *Handbook of aging and the social sciences.* New York: Van Nostrand Reinhold.

Sutton, G. (1980). Assortive marriages for smoking habits. *Annals of Human Biology, 7,* 449-456.

Swartz, D. R. (1984). Dealing with chronic illness in childhood. *Pediatrics in Review, 6,* 67-73.

Tolle, S. W., & Girard, D. E. (1983). The physician's role in the events surrounding patient death. *Archives of Internal Medicine, 143,* 1447-1449.

Tolle, S. W., Bascom, P. B., Hickam, D. H., & Benson, J. A. (1986). Communication between physicians and surviving spouses following patient deaths. *Journal of General Internal Medicine, 1,* 309-314.

Tolle, S. W., Elliot, D. L., & Hickam, D. H. (1984). Physician attitudes and practices at the time of patient death. *Achives of Internal Medicine, 144,* 2389-2391.

Tolle, S. W., & Girard, D. W. (1983). The physician's role in the events surrounding patient death. *Archives of Internal Medicine, 143,* 1447-1449.

Turk, D. C., & Kerns, R. D. (Eds.). (1985). *Health, illness, and families: A life-span perspective.* New York: John Wiley.

Turk, D. C., Litt, M. D., & Salovey, P. (1985). Seeking urgent pediatric treatment: Factors contributing to frequency, delay, and appropriateness. *Health Psychology, 4,* 43-59.

Tyroler, H. A., Johnson, A. L., & Fulton, J. T. (1965). Patterns of preventive health behavior in populations. *Journal of Health and Human Behavior, 6,* 128-140.

U.S. Department of Commerce. (1980). *Statistical Abstracts of the United States* (101s.d.S.P.-25,N.802,888). Washington, DC: Government Printing Office.

U.S. Department of Health, Education & Welfare. (1976). *Teenage smoking, national patterns of cigarette smoking, ages 12-18, in 1972 & 1974,* DHEW Publication No. (NIH) 76-931. Bethesda, MD: NIH.

van der Veen, F. (1965). The parent's concept of the family unit and child adjustment. *Journal of Consulting Psychology, 12,* 196-200.

Ramsey, C. N., Abell, T. D., & Baker, L. C. (1986). The relationship between family functioning, life events, family structure and the outcome of pregnancy. *Journal of Family Practice, 22,* 521-527.

Vaughn, C. E., & Leff, L. P. (1976). The influence of family and social factors on the course of psychiatric illness: A comparison of schizophrenic and depressed neurotic patients. *British Journal of Psychiatry, 129*, 125-137.

Venters, M. H., Jacobs, D. R., Luepker, R. V., Maiman, L. A., & Gillum, R. F. (1984). Spouse concordance of smoking patterns: The Minnesota heart survey. *American Journal of Epidemiology, 120*, 608-616.

Verbrugge, L. M. (1977). Marital status and health. *Journal of Marriage and the Family, 7*, 267-285.

Walker, G. (1983). The pact: The caretaker-parent/ill-child coalition in families with chronic illness. *Family Systems Medicine, 1*, 6-29.

Wasow, M. (1985). Chronic schizophrenia and Alzheimer's disease: The losses for parents, spouses and children compared. *Journal of Chronic Disease, 38*, 711-716.

Watzlawick, P., & Coyne, J. C. (1980). Depression following stroke: Brief, problem-focused family treatment. *Family Process, 19*, 13-18.

Weakland, J. H. (1977). Family somatics: A neglected edge. *Family Process, 16*, 263-272.

Weakland, J. H., & Fisch, R. (1984). Cases that "don't make sense": Brief strategic treatment in medical practice. *Family Systems Medicine, 2*, 125-136.

Weiss, S. T., Tager, T. B., Schenker, M., & Speizer, F. E. (1983). The health effects of involuntary smoking. *Annual Review of Respiratory Disease, 128*, 933-942.

Wellisch, D. K., Mosher, M. B., & Van Scoy, C. (1978). Management of family emotion stress: Family group therapy in a private oncology practice. *International Journal of Group Psychotherapy, 28*, 225-232.

West, D. W., Graham, S., Swanson, M., & Wilkinson, G. (1977). Five year follow-up of a smoking withdrawal clinic population. *American Journal of Public Health, 67*, 536-544.

White, K., Kolman, M. L., Wexler, P., Polin, G., & Winter, R. J. (1984). Unstable diabetes and unstable families: A psychosocial evaluation of diabetic children with recurrent ketoacidosis. *Pediatrics, 73*, 749-755.

Wilber, J. A., & Barrows, J. S. (1972). Hypertension—a community problem. *American Journal of Medicine, 52*, 653-663.

Williams, R. M., Lane, J. D., Kuhn, C. M. et al. (1982). Type A behavior and elevated physiological and neuroendocrine responses to cognitive tasks. *Science, 218*, 483-485.

Wilson, G. T., & Brownell, K. (1978). Behavior therapy for obesity: Including family members in the treatment process. *Behavior Therapy, 9*, 943-945.

Wishner, W. J., & O'Brien, M. D. (1978). Diabetes and the family. *Medical Clinics of North America, 62*, 849-856.

Wright, L. M., & Leahey, M. (1984). *Nurses and families*. Philadelphia: F. A. Davis.

Wynne, L. C., & Singer, M. T. (1963a). Thought disorder and family relations of schizophrenics. I. A research study. *Archives of General Psychiatry, 9*, 191-198.

Wynne, L. C., & Singer, M. T. (1963b). Thought disorder and family relations of schizophrenics. II. A classification of forms of thinking. *Archives of General Psychiatry, 9*, 199-206.

Zola, I. K. (1972). Studying the decision to see a doctor. *Advances in Psychosomatic Medicine, 8*, 216-236.

Zuckerman, D. M., Kasl, S. V., & Ostfeld, A. M. (1984). Psychosocial predictors of mortality among the elderly poor: The role of religion, well-being, and social contact. *American Journal of Epidemiology, 119*, 410-423.

Author Index

Subject Index

157

About the Authors

William J. Doherty received his Ph.D. in family studies from the University of Connecticut in 1978. Since then, he has spent most of his career working in family medicine departments at the University of Iowa and the University of Oklahoma. In 1986, he joined the faculty of the Family Social Science Department at the University of Minnesota, where he teaches and does research on family and health issues. He also holds a faculty appointment in the Department of Family Practice and Community Health at the University of Minnesota's medical school. An active marriage and family therapist, he has coauthored and coedited three other books in the field: *Family Therapy and Family Medicine: Toward the Primary Care of Families* (with Macaran A. Baird); *Family-Centered Medical Care: A Clinical Casebook* (with Macaran A. Baird); and *Family Medicine: The Maturing of a Discipline* (with Charles Christianson and Marvin Sussman).

Thomas L. Campbell received his undergraduate degree from Harvard College and his M.D. (1979) from Harvard Medical School. He completed his family practice residency and his fellowship in psychosomatic medicine at the University of Rochester School of Medicine and Dentistry. Since 1983, he has been Assistant Professor of Family Medicine and Psychiatry at the University of Rochester, where he teaches family systems medicine to family practice residents. His interests include the role of the family in medical practice and research on the influence of the family on physical and mental health. He recently wrote a monograph, *Family's Impact on Health*, for the National Institute of Mental Health. He is board certified in family practice and a member of the Society of Teachers of Family Medicine.

NOTES